Basic Domestic Pet Library

Housebreaking & Training Puppies
A Complete and Up-to-Date Guide

Approved by the A.S.P.C.A.

J.R. Gardner

Published in association with T.F.H. Publications, Inc.,
the world's largest and most respected publisher of pet literature

Chelsea House Publishers
Philadelphia

Basic Domestic Pet Library

A Cat in the Family
Amphibians Today
Aquarium Beautiful
Choosing the Perfect Cat
Dog Obedience Training
Dogs: Selecting the Best Dog for You
Ferrets Today
Guppies Today
Hamsters Today
Housebreaking and Training Puppies
Iguanas in Your Home
Kingsnakes & Milk Snakes
Kittens Today
Lovebirds Today
Parakeets Today
Pot-bellied Pigs
Rabbits Today
Turtles Today

Publisher's Note: All of the photographs in this book have been coated with FOTOGLAZE™ finish, a special lamination that imparts a new dimension of colorful gloss to the photographs.

Reinforced Library Binding & Super-Highest Quality Boards

This edition © 1997 Chelsea House Publishers, a division of Main Line Book Company

© yearBOOKS, Inc.

1 3 5 7 9 8 6 4 2   3 9082 07063578 7

Library of Congress Cataloging-in-Publication Data

Gardner, J. R.
    Housebreaking and training puppies : a complete and up-to-date
guide / J.R. Gardner.
        p.   cm. -- (Basic domestic pet library)
    "Approved by the A.S.P.C.A."
    Includes index.
    ISBN 0-7910-4610-9 (hardcover)
    1. Puppies--Training.   I. American Society for the Prevention of
Cruelty to Animals. II. Title. III. Series.
SF431.G36   1997
636.7'0835--dc21   97-4182
                                                            CIP

HOUSEBREAKING AND TRAINING A PUPPY

a yearBOOK by J. R. Gardner

yearBOOKS,INC.
Dr. Herbert R. Axelrod
Founder & Chairman

Neal Pronek
Chief Editor

Andrew De Prisco
Editor

yearBOOKS are all photo composed, color separated and designed on Scitex equipment in Neptune, N.J. with the following staff:

COMPUTER ART
  Michael L. Secord
    Supervisor
  Sherise Buhagiar
  Patti Escabi
  Cynthia Fleureton
  Sandra Taylor Gale
  Pat Marotta
  Joanne Muzyka
  Robert Onyrscuk
  Tom Roberts

Advertising Sales
George Campbell
  Chief
Amy Manning
  Coordinator

Photo credits: Paulette Braun, Isabelle Francais, Corinna Kamer, Robert Pearcy, Karen Taylor.

Who can deny the ever-growing popularity of dogs in our world? We can approximate that 250,000 puppies are born each year that will need good owners and proper training. That's a lot of dog kibble, wee-wee pads, and patience to bring up each new generation of puppies. Fortunately there are thousands of dog professionals --- specialists, behaviorists, trainers, breeders, handlers, etc. --- in the world constantly breaking new grounds in their fields. It seems that no world is expanding as rapidly as the dog world, and how tough it is to stay on top of the latest developments, trends, products, and the like. This Puppy Training yearBOOK is designed to help you stay abreast of what's new and eye-opening, so that your puppy and you can profit from the best knowledge and advice.

What are YearBOOKS?

Because keeping dogs as pets continues to grow at a rapid pace, information on the training of puppies is vitally needed in the marketplace. Books, the usual way information of this sort is transmitted, can be too slow. Sometimes by the time a book is written and published, the material contained therein is a year or two old...and no new material has been added during that time. Only a book in a magazine form can bring breaking stories and current information. A magazine is streamlined in production, so we have adopted certain magazine publishing techniques in the creation of this yearBOOK. Magazines also can be much cheaper than books because they are supported by advertising. To combine these assets into a great publication, we issued this yearBOOK in both magazine and book format at different prices.

CONTENTS

IT ALL BEGINS WITH BONDING

There is a tendency within certain of the more recent training books and magazine articles to suggest that bonding is some sort of new concept in training. How untrue! Bonding has been the basis of good training techniques through the centuries. Recently, however, its importance has gained greater recognition in today's approach to puppy training.

WHAT IS BONDING?

By developing a strong bond with your puppy, certain doors can be opened. If you have a strong bond with your dog, it will be more willing to accept discipline from you without being at risk to negative side effects. It will trust in you and will allow you to take care of its daily needs as well as to inspect its teeth, or examine its paws, or stand over it without feeling threatened or intimidated. The all-important aspect in respect of bonding is that it creates trust.

But bonding is not just about love and fuss and all things nice, it is also about mutual respect: this aspect is sometimes forgotten. Without respect, the end result is not true bonding, but a one-way flow of fuss that makes for the beginnings of a totally spoilt pet. The pet does all the taking and you do all the giving—that is not bonding in my understanding of the term. You may read elsewhere that bonding must be achieved before any training can begin.

Well, I can tell you this just is not so unless you are dealing with a wild animal that you want to tame, or a puppy or adult with emotional problems.

Never forget that when you are bonding or training a puppy, you are not dealing just with a dog, or a breed, you are dealing with a living organism that is a unique individual—it is as complex in its psychological make-up as you

Puppies must NEVER be left alone with very young children. The children might hurt the puppies, or vice versa, without understanding what they are doing. Having a painful experience with a child might turn a puppy's love to fear.

and I are. You cannot talk to it, so you must communicate your thoughts and intentions in a way it understands, which is via the most universal language on earth—by your very actions, your voice, and your demeanor.

When you obtain a puppy it will have received some form of socialization. What you must therefore do is to go heavy on the fuss, and easy on the discipline until the puppy knows where it stands with you. You cannot allow the puppy to do just what it wants otherwise you are encouraging problems later on. Its own mother has been very gentle with it, but she has not let it run riot by the time it is over four weeks old. Such a puppy is quite capable of learning more than its young age might suggest. This does not mean it can learn advanced obedience and tricks at this age, but it can learn good manners and what it can and cannot do.

How to Bond with Your Puppy

Forming a bond with a puppy is an easy task. The basic social instincts of a dog predispose it to want a relationship with you, its pack leader, and other members of your pack which hold a higher rank than it does. You, of course, must assume the pack leader role. The bonding will be in two forms, touch and sound.

Touch: It is very important that your puppy is touched very often in a gentle soothing manner. Do not concentrate your touch just to its head and back, but extend this to its entire body, meaning its legs, its paws, tail, chest and belly. It will especially enjoy your scratching behind its ears, its chest, and its back at the root

Playing with puppies at an early age bonds them to humans. Experiments in Germany have shown that dogs raised without human bonding behave like wild wolves.

of its tail. When it is in a subdued mood—just before it has a nap—you can place it on your knee and gently scratch behind its ears and this will have a very soothing, almost hypnotic, effect on most puppies.

At this time you can gently lift its lip up in order to inspect its teeth. You are not doing a physical check up but merely getting the pup familiar with the touch of your hand on every part of its body, so only do this momentarily on its lips. Likewise, you can hold its ear and stroke the inside flap. Stroke the sides of its body and flanks. This is all there is to physical bonding, so it is a case of doing it as often as possible.

You should get down on your knees and play with your puppy, let it lick your face by all means as this is a quite natural submissive gesture that it would do with older members of the pack. It's just fine for it to clamber all over you and paw at you just as it would with its siblings and the older members of the pack. Take care, however, that you are not too rough with the puppy, and be especially watchful of young children in the household. They must not be allowed to pull on or drag the puppy about. This sort of action will result in either a very timid or a very aggressive dog in later months. Too many adults allow their children to maul their pets. This must be discouraged.

You should not stare at your puppy or in any way force it to maintain eye contact with you. This would represent an aggressive gesture to a puppy by an adult and will intimidate the youngster. Whenever the puppy looks you straight in the eyes, you should talk to it cheerfully and softly.

Vocal Bonding: Never underestimate the power of vocalizations in bonding with your puppy or adult dog. You would think nothing of talking gibberish to a human baby. In this matter puppies are similar to humans, as are most animals. Of course, there is no need to talk gibberish but do talk to your puppy as often as you can. However, always remember that your puppy will not understand a word you say, so your tone of voice is the important thing.

Your dog is able to understand the volume, tone and length of words. When you call the puppy to you, use a higher tone and an excited manner so as to arouse its curiosity. When it reaches you, continue to sound excited and really pleased that the puppy came. Much praise is in order at this time. In the wild, when dogs meet or prepare for a hunt, there is much physical contact and excitement, and this is also shown in their vocalizations. At other times you should speak softly to your puppy so that it is

From a practical point of view, selling house-trained puppies is a lot easier than selling untrained puppies—plus new owners appreciate not having the chore of housebreaking.

reassured of your affection for it. When you take it for a walk, draw its attention to things on the ground and it will inspect these and maybe paw at them or the ground. What you are doing by such actions is involving the puppy with you. If it stops to inspect something, you do likewise and ask it what it is. If your friends see you conducting such a conversation and think you are going a little nuts, that's okay. Some of the greatest men and women down the ages did just this with their pets. Apart from this, you will get much more out of your pup than such friends ever will from theirs.

Your voice is your most valuable training tool. You can't always touch or pull your puppy. There will be many times when you will have to call your puppy, perhaps even to stop him from running onto a busy street. This nine-week-old female German Shorthair is owned by Delwood Miller.

Your voice will come to be the singular most powerful training aid you have because, unlike touch, it is effective when your dog is at a distance. Likewise, arm movements are also an extremely important means of communication with your dog when it is at a distance, so by all means use them from the outset. If the puppy is doing something it should not, say no in a drawn out way. Initially you should use this command only when the puppy is very close to you, or when you can get to it quickly. As the puppy bonds with you so you are able to put more bite into the volume and tone.

Never Risk Frightening the Puppy

Everything about bonding must be done on a steady build-up basis and in such a way that there is never a risk that you might frighten the puppy. For example, if you see the puppy doing something wrong, such as pulling on drapes or the furniture, you should approach it as quickly as you can, but not so quickly that you startle it into flight. Never lunge down at it to pick it up, but do this slowly. Always let your puppy see what you intend to do. This becomes crucially important if you do not have a thorough knowledge of how the puppy was treated in its previous home.

Even if the pup came from a very good source, you must understand that when it moves into your home it is in effect changing from one pack to another. Everything is strange, so it has to be assured that it is totally safe with you and can trust that you are its new protector and

Never scare or frighten a puppy or bonding may be impossible. You need only look at your puppy's face to see if it's frightened or not.

leader. This early bonding period should extend to every member of the household, and to visitors as well, because this will have a lasting effect on all that follows.

Bonding is not something that is restricted by a time frame. It commences the very day you collect the puppy and continues throughout its life. Its progress will depend heavily on how much time you spend with the puppy. If it is left alone for long periods this will most certainly have a very negative effect on both its ability to be trained and in the amount it can learn. This is why if all of the family are out for most of the day, it is not actually the sort of environment conducive to bringing up a puppy.

With the average puppy you should be able to achieve a high level of bonding within a few days, perhaps taking somewhat longer if the puppy is from a bad home. With an older dog, say one from a rescue shelter, you must approach bonding very carefully because simple acts that present no problem with a puppy may frighten or threaten an adult. For example, placing your arm around a puppy should result in only pleasure for the puppy—but it could be an extremely threatening action to a dog that has been mistreated.

Bonding and Mutual Respect

With the average puppy there should be no problems in teaching it respect as it bonds with you. Indeed, this is an important part of its learning process. Teaching it to respect you does not mean punishing in any harsh sense, but simply that it must learn very quickly that certain actions are not acceptable in its new pack. For example, if it starts to nip too hard on your hand, or to bite and pull at your trousers, or to jump on a chair, then this must be corrected on the spot.

It must always be remembered that in the wild a puppy would learn many things concurrently. If you attempt to teach your pup one thing at a time, this merely allows more time for unwanted behaviors to become established and reinforced as part of the behavior. The only time that thorough bonding should be achieved before discipline is when you are dealing with a puppy that you know has been subjected to bad treatment in previous hands.

Associations between people and puppies should be like associations between human friends. There must be mutual trust and respect or the friendship gets nowhere. You earn respect by letting your puppy know what is right or wrong from the beginning. Changing behavior is very difficult; early training is simple and necessary. You can't train a puppy without spending time with it. Owner, Janice Bykowsky.

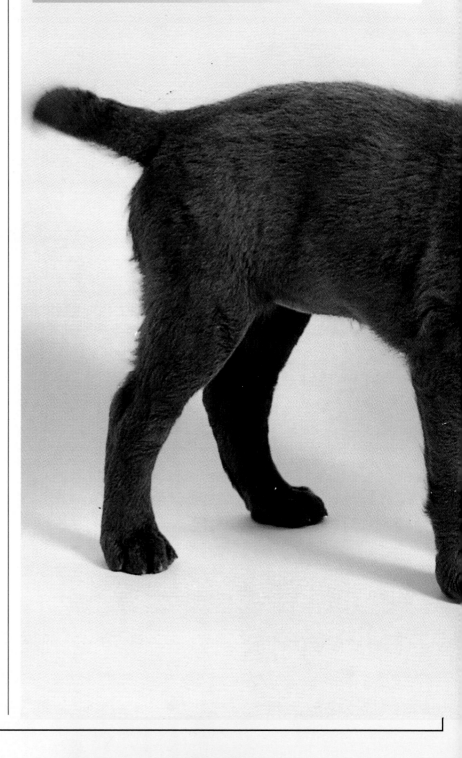

With large breeds like this Great Dane, it is an absolute necessity to train the puppy. Even in play, an untrained or disobedient Great Dane could be dangerous to a child who might be playing with it. Owners, Rick and Judy Abrams.

A MATTER OF DISCIPLINE

The subject of discipline is a bed of thorns for an author. Unlike the situation when a trainer meets a client, the author cannot make any assessment of either the owner or the dog to be trained, or which already has problems. You may have just purchased your puppy, or you may have had it some months, or maybe you have acquired an older dog and find that it has some undesirable habits which you wish to correct.

Always bear in mind that every dog is an individual, every person is likewise, and every environment (home and location) differs from any other. When you consider the permutations of these three factors, you will appreciate that no author can presuppose you and your pet are of this or that type. It is a case of your understanding the underlying principles and applying them to your needs.

WHAT DOES DISCIPLINE MEAN?

Discipline means applying whatever level of punishment is needed in order to establish total control over your dog. It is the application of a negative stimulus of sufficient level that it is greater than the reinforcer that works to maintain a given pattern of behavior. You have learned that your puppy adopts you and your family as a pack. It is important that in order for the puppy to be happily, and safely, integrated in the pack, its position in the social hierarchy is at the bottom.

Your puppy does not think that being at the bottom of the pack is in any way demeaning. Life is not so complex for it. Its sole object in life is to survive with the least amount of problems and in the most comfortable manner it can. Within this framework it will endeavor to get as much of its

There can be no pleasurable relationship between you and your dog if he isn't trained to obey. This dog has retrieved a Nylabone® Frisbee™ (that's the one with a bone molded into the top and made of extra strong polyurethane) and won't give it up. General training will enable you to control your dog in situations like this where a firm NO! will make the dog stop whatever it is doing. Photo courtesy of Nylabone, Ltd., England.

own way as it can. Your sole objective as a pack leader is to limit its power in such a way that it is contented with its role within society.

If you own a breed of dog that will grow up to be large, and especially if it is of the traditional guarding breeds, such as the Rottweiler, German Shepherd, Doberman, Boxer, Mastiff and the like, and you do not have total control over your dog, you are being totally irresponsible and dangerous to society.

If your puppy is of a small to medium-sized breed, this can also be true. Remember, in every little dog there is a big dog trying to get out! Small canines are just as capable of wanting to be the boss. They may never be as potentially dangerous as a large breed, but they can still be a real nuisance and can badly frighten children or the elderly. When you obtain your puppy, you assume the commitment of a leader, so you have a moral obligation to stick to your end of that commitment.

this than to allow your dog to become uncontrollable and thus dangerous. The saying "spare the rod and spoil the child" still has application, even in this day and age, to children that simply do not react to verbal warnings.

Your puppy is no different, indeed, as it will never reach the age of reason it must be allowed to learn from its own mistakes. Deny it this and you deny it the opportunity to be as

transgress the rules.

Discipline must be used fairly and consistently at all times. Bear in mind that your dog will constantly try to "test" your resolve. Give in once and it will push for a second, then a third time. Eventually it will respond to you only when it feels so inclined, and maybe not at all. If you then decide to "put your foot down," you just might find you have a defiant dog on your hands that will stand its ground and really challenge you. Back down from this situation and you can just bet the next one will be when your dog actually bites you as it challenges you.

Of course, we all allow our pets to get away with something or other, after all, to err is human. The main thing is that in the important aspects of its life your dog must be totally obedient. In determining any course of corrective action you should always bear in mind a number of important rules:

This Mastiff puppy is being taught to retrieve. Every time he brings the dental device back to his master, he is rewarded with affection and praise.

The Use of Discipline

A sufficient level of a stimulus, the key to effective discipline and training, can range merely from the tone of your voice to a hard spanking, depending on the behavior pattern and the circumstances. Physical punishment should always be the very last resort that you use but, and this is important, it is better to use

natural as it can be within a domestic framework. You must be the pack leader, and your puppy must grow up to recognize this reality. If you train your puppy correctly, the need for physical punishment, other than in the most mild form, will never be needed. If your puppy is taught at an early age how to respond to basic commands, it will rarely

1. Discipline must be given at the time of the transgression. Work on the basis that such correction will be associated in the dog's mind by the thing it is doing at the time of the punishment, or was doing 20 seconds earlier at the most.
2. While the punishment should be sufficient to register a point in the mind of the dog, it must never be excessive. This serves no purpose and may create a fear situation.
3. The general temperament of your dog must be considered when determining punishment. A quiet gentle dog should never need more than strong verbal admonishment. A bold and defiant

An English Bulldog puppy chewing on a Gumabone® Wishbone. With strong chewers like Bulldogs, safe chewing devices are necessary. Nylabones® cost more but they are made from virgin materials and are safer and last longer. This puppy is enjoying his chewing very much. Unless he is properly trained, he might bite your hand if you tried to take it away from him. Obviously you wouldn't take his Gumabone® away, but if he was chewing on something dangerous, taking it away quickly might be a dangerous thing to do.

Doberman Pinscher puppies are cute when young, but they are strong and can be real nuisances if they are untrained. No dog is trainable when it is very hungry or must urgently relieve itself.

ties that come to know each other on an intimate basis so that each can almost read the other's mind. This can only happen against a background where there is both affection and respect.

Disciplinary Tools

There are a number of tools available to you which may be needed in educating your puppy into the ways of living within a human environment. I will mention a number of these, including some that I personally would never use, even though some trainers have recommended their effectiveness. In each instance I will suggest its use and its drawbacks.

"No" Command: This will be your most effective tool because it has the dual virtues of being with you all of the time and is effective even when the puppy or dog is at some distance from you. Further, it has no negative side effects because it does not involve physical discomfort for the puppy, only the threat of this if an action is not stopped.

Throw Chain: This is a choke collar of suitable weight for the the dog. Its merit is that it can be used when the dog is not at hand but when it is within reasonable distance. It works on the basis of startling the dog rather than hurting it. It must only ever be thrown at the rear end of the dog, so there is never any risk of injuring it, as might be the case if it hits its head. Its disadvantage is that you must be very sure it hits the dog when it is thrown.

Alternatives to the throw chain which work on the same principle are a bunch of keys, an empty aluminum soft

dog is going to need an equally bold and assertive owner.

4. You should never punish your dog if you are in a bad mood. If you do, it is highly probable that this will be greater than is needed.

5. Always ponder whether there is an alternative method of correcting a behavior pattern before resorting to physical punishment.

6. Try to avoid any situation where you cannot enforce a given command if need be. If your dog gets it into its mind that you are not able to enforce a command, it may well decide to continue doing what it wants to do rather than what you want it to do.

7. Never forget that in certain situations neither verbal commands, nor even hard punishment, will correct a behavior pattern if it is created either by hunger, or because it attempts to stop a trait that is highly inherent. If a dog's problem is created by hunger, you must address this first of all. If the problem is the result of contrasting thresholds, as seen in some breeds that persist in fighting other dogs, the answer may well be that removal of reinforcer is the only acceptable and reliable solution.

8. Training your puppy is not something that you should turn on and off only when a problem is met. It is an ongoing process throughout the life of the dog. It is the blending of two personali-

drinks can with a few pebbles or marbles in it, and a water pistol. A more severe tool would be a slingshot, but this is even less reliable for the average person and is potentially more dangerous to your pet.

Choke Chain: This may range from spiked to merely a smooth-linked chain. It is used in order to gain a quicker response from a puller when teaching a puppy to walk correctly on a leash. It makes life a little easier for you if a large dog is on the other end of the lead, but even then some dogs may happily pull against the choke if they are not correctly trained as a puppy.

Long Line: This is useful in teaching a dog to respond to sit and stay instructions. It works on the basis that if the dog ignores the command and runs away, it will quite suddenly be upended when it reaches the end of the line. It may also be used for a number of other behavioral problems.

Balloons and Mousetraps: These are used in order to dissuade a dog from reclining in your chairs. They may not always be effective because some dogs are smart enough to only go on the chair when they see these or similar objects are not there!

Electric Collars: These work on the basis that the dog receives a mild electric shock when it transgresses at a distance from you. I have never used one, nor would I recommend the average pet owner to do so. There are many potentially negative side effects, such as aversion to any form of collar, to stress and frustration inducement that might manifest itself in unwanted patterns of behavior, including aggression. Ultrasonic sound wave appliances are also promoted by some trainers. Again, I have little confidence in any training aid that I am not totally sure how it may affect the mind, and thus behavior of a dog.

Lead, Strap, or Similar Item: The use of a lead or strap has been a tool of discipline for centuries. Its advantage is that it is convenient in that it will be with you when you are out with your dog and is effective if used correctly. Its drawback is that if used incorrectly, the dog may associate it only with punishment. Overall, I would not recommend its use.

Shaking or Lifting: This, along with the final corrective tool, is what I call a natural means of administering discipline. Little physical pain is felt, but when you hold a dog by the scruff of the neck and shake it while issuing a verbal command, the dog will apply its whole attention to what you are saying. It is akin to a mother dog's grabbing and shaking her puppy, which is how a puppy is taught. When a puppy is lifted from the floor, it is placed in a vulnerable position that it does not like. Again, as a result, it will concentrate on what else is happening. If you are saying no in a stern voice, it will associate the action it was doing with the

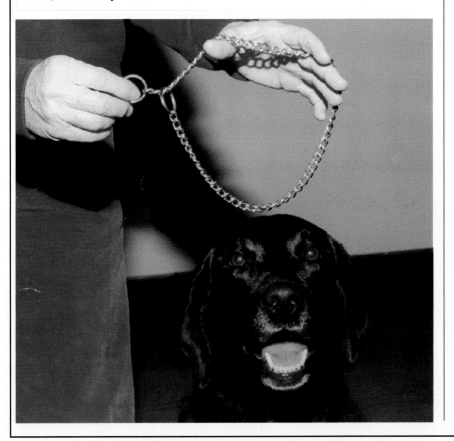

This black Labrador Retriever about to be fitted with a choke collar. There is disagreement about using choke collars as they are dangerous and not especially kind. They are, however, very effective in training larger dogs not to pull when you are walking them. Photo of Marsh Dak's Shooting Star, CD, owned by Dianne L. Schlemmer.

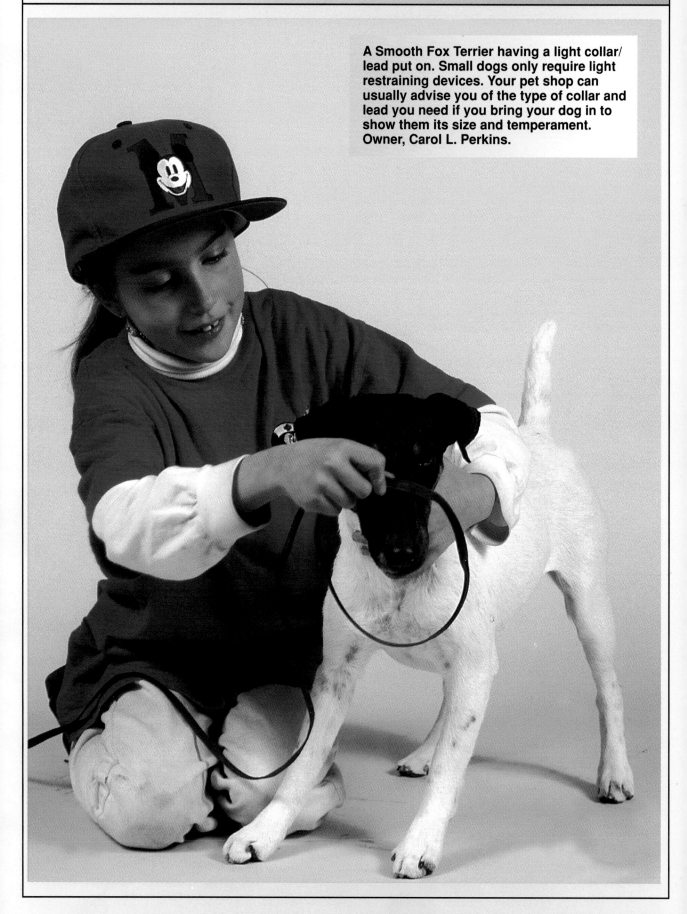

A Smooth Fox Terrier having a light collar/lead put on. Small dogs only require light restraining devices. Your pet shop can usually advise you of the type of collar and lead you need if you bring your dog in to show them its size and temperament. Owner, Carol L. Perkins.

consequence (shaking)and the word no. Thereafter, the word no is associated with the punishment, so the shaking is rarely needed.

The Ultimate Natural Aid—Your Hand: This has the advantage that it is the only tool, other than your voice, that is sure to always be with you! Much has been written about not using your hand to administer discipline to your dog, so I will try and put matters into some sort of perspective based on years of experience with dogs and many other animals. I regard the hand as the most obvious, effective, and least unreliable aid that I have. It is as natural for me to use as a dog its teeth, a cat its claws, or a horse its hoofs. Out there in the real world it undoubtedly remains the most used tool by dog owners. The argument against it as a means of administering discipline is that the pet will become hand-shy. If this happens, then it suggests it has been used inappropriately. Further, even if you use a strap or switch you will still raise your hand in order to use it, so the dog can still become hand-shy.

When a dog is bitten by another dog, it does not make it fearful of muzzling the same or other dogs under different conditions. When a cat is scratched by another cat, it does not make it fearful of the paws of other cats. The same is also true of a horse that is bitten or kicked by another horse. What each of these learns is that the teeth, paws, or hoofs can be instruments of punishment *if* the occasion demands this. The operative word is "if."

If a dog, cat, or a horse is

Training Rottweilers is easy because they are a fairly intelligent breed. Don't be afraid to use your hands in as gentle a manner as possible to train your dog. Regardless of what some experts say, your hand and your voice are your most valuable tools in training your dog. Owner, Lori Rizzitano.

always striking out at its peers for virtually no reason, then of course its fellows will tend to avoid getting too near to it. If you spank your dog at the very slightest provocation, then it is to be expected that it will become very wary of your hand. But if it only associates your hand with a spanking when it has ignored a verbal command, then it has no reason to fear the hand under any other situation. Your hand is part of you, and it is you that the dog must have the utmost respect for.

This means it must learn that if it gives you no reason to

get annoyed with it, life will be trouble-free and filled with affection. If it ignores you, it will experience problems of discomfort for its transgression. Indeed, this is as near to the natural way in which it would learn as it can within a human pack.

Just remember that your hand is no different to any other training aid if it is used incorrectly: it will create fear, and frustration. It is not so much the tool that is so important in disciplining your dog as the consistency, the extent of punishment, and the timing.

When bringing your puppy home, you will need chew toys. Every puppy must chew! Buy the safest chew devices available from your local pet shop. The best known products are made by the Nylabone® Co. They have been around for more than 40 years and, while their products may be more expensive, they last much longer because they are made from virgin nylon and polyurethane. DON'T OFFER YOUR PUPPY ANYTHING SOFT WHICH IT CAN SWALLOW AND CHOKE!! Owner, Camelots American Staffordshire Terriers.

WHAT EQUIPMENT WILL YOU NEED?

In an ideal world you are reading this section *before* you obtain your puppy. This might save you some wasted money spent on inferior products. If you already have the puppy, there are probably a number of items you may not yet have purchased, but which will certainly be worthwhile investments. Keep in mind, the best equipment is invariably the cheapest in the long run, so try to purchase top-quality supplies from the outset.

PUPPY IDENTIFICATION

One of the first things you should obtain for your puppy is some form of identification so if it is lost you can be notified. It is surprising just how many pups and adults become totally lost because their owners just did not fit a tag or other means of identification. The options are collar plates, loose tags fitted to the collar, and tattoos. The latter is easily the best choice because it is permanent. I hate to mention this but a number of lost or stolen puppies and adults can end up in experimental laboratories. Establishments are loathe to accept tattooed dogs because these indicate the owner wanted the dog permanently identified. Those who steal puppies will usually discard tattooed animals because they can be traced. Your vet can attend to this. A number is placed inside the rear thigh or inside the ear;

When puppies are raised with other animals in the same house, they usually identify with them as individuals. This means that a puppy and kitten in YOUR home might get along well, but a strange dog would probably have problems with the same kitten. In any case, having pets of different species is always interesting.

the thigh is preferred. You can use your social security number, or other personal ID, and this is registered with one of the national associations. A loose tag is also supplied. If you opt for collar ID, it is best to have a collar that features a metal plate that can be engraved. Loose tags can easily come off.

FEEDING BOWLS

You will need three feeding bowls for your pet. One for water, one for soft foods, such as canned meats, and one for dry dog biscuits. The shape and size of the bowls should of course reflect the size and breed of your puppy. The ear type should also be a consideration. If you have a very long flop-eared breed, you do not want its ears dangling in the food and water bowls as it eats or drinks, so choose a size that will be less likely for this to happen. If you have a tall breed, or a breed with a long

not so readily picked up by a puppy and chewed when the pup is going through its teething period (two to six months of age). They are also more readily cleaned as they age than are plastic dishes, which tend to get scratched, and stainless steel can be sterilized. Water bowls should be cleaned and replenished on a daily basis. Should this not

discarded once the puppy has satiated itself. By leaving moist food down you not only increase the risk that flies will contaminate it but you will tend to encourage the puppy to be a picky eater, which of course becomes a behavior pattern that results in the puppy's pestering you for food.

Given that insufficient food can become the source of many

Have you ever seen anything more beautiful than a litter of trained Lhasa Apso puppies posing for a prospective buyer? When feeding time comes, you better have one bowl for each unless you feed them at separate times. Owner, Linda Jarrett.

neck, you may wish to purchase a stand for the bowls so that the puppy doesn't have to exert himself to eat and drink.

Crock (earthenware) or stainless steel bowls are the best choice because they are

be done, there is always the chance that when the puppy grows tall enough it might start drinking from your toilet because this is fresher than the water you have left for it!

Any leftover canned foods should be removed and

unwanted behaviors, such as stealing, and of syndromes, such as copro- and geophagia (fecal and soil eating), it is most important that the feeding regimen of a puppy is satisfactory. The latter syndromes often commence

More important than any equipment or supplies, your new puppy needs love and attention. Shar-Pei owned by Alice Lawler.

with puppies and may persist into adult life if the problem is not corrected rapidly.

GROOMING TOOLS

Regular grooming is an important part of dog management. It is absolutely essential for the longhaired breeds. It requires that you touch all parts of your puppy, and this is good for bonding between you. It enables you to inspect the skin of the dog for parasites. Apart from the illnesses they can create, fleas and lice can of course cause irritation that can lead to habitual skin biting even after the parasites have been eradicated.

In the case of the breeds that need their coats trimmed, such as Poodles, Bedlingtons, spaniels and terriers, the inability of many owners to groom their pets is but one stage that can lead to the pet becoming aggressive in other patterns of behavior. Apart from this aspect, by being unable to groom these breeds, the owners merely make life so much more difficult for the professional groomer when his or her services are needed. Further, the whole grooming process becomes unpleasant for many dogs.

If your dog will not allow you to groom it because you have let its coat become a matted mess, the dog may take its victory over you in this matter to the next situation. It knows that if it shows defiance you may give in, so it will certainly test you in one or more ways. Because it will not let you groom it, it may take the same attitude when it goes to a salon and become extremely aggressive with the groomer.

A Silky Terrier puppy requires as much training as a Great Dane which might be 50 times heavier. It also requires careful grooming as do most long-haired breeds. It is impossible for the owner to groom his dog if it is undisciplined. Owners, M.L. and Sarah Stegemann.

Four Paws offers an extensive line of grooming brushes, from slickers to curry brushes to pin brushes. They have a brush to suit the grooming needs of every breed of dog. These brushes are available at your local pet shop. Photo courtesy of Four Paws.

every 12 weeks at the least. If you cannot afford such regular attention to these breeds, do not purchase them in the first place, or be real sure you can cope with grooming.

For the average non-heavy-coated breed, you will need one wide- and one narrow-toothed comb. Those made of steel are the best and should have a handle. A stiff non-nylon brush is preferred to plastic. Obtain one with bristle length and stiffness appropriate to your dog's adult coat. Very soft brushes are a waste of time, even on smooth-coated breeds. A slicker brush is recommended if you have a trimmed, stripped, or heavy-coated breed. It is rectangular in shape with a handle from

It is no fun for a Poodle, a terrier, or a spaniel with a long matted coat to be trimmed. Matters are often made worse because the owners will persist in bathing their dogs without being able to groom them. This simply makes the mats harder to deal with, especially on the legs, which are the most delicate part to groom in the first place.

If you cannot cope with grooming your longhaired breed, at least give it a good brushing. When grooming, you place the dog in a situation where it may challenge your authority. But if you do not groom your longhaired, high-maintenance dog, you must seek a professional's services on a regular basis. Begin this when still a puppy. A Poodle will need trimming every six to eight weeks—never let it go beyond this time. A terrier or a Cocker Spaniel will need stripping or trimming about

For breeds that require clipping, the tool of choice is the electric clipper. Grooming kits are the answer to solving the pet grooming problems. Pet shops offer the highest quality grooming aids available. Photo courtesy of Wahl.

the back at an angle. The pins are relatively short and made of wire, set into a stiff pad. This brush will remove tangles and should be used before a comb. There are plastic slickers but these are not as good as those with wire pins. The long-pinned brushes set into a soft rubber pad have limited use because they give way so readily to any obstruction in the coat. A silk, chamois, or similar cloth is useful to place a sheen on the short-coated breed.

If you commence grooming your puppy from the time you obtain it, you will experience few problems. One of the most common errors made by owners is that they press too hard with a comb on sensitive areas of the body—legs, tail, abdomen and ears. Never pull hard on tangles—tease them out with your fingers, then brush, then wide comb, then fine comb until they are removed. The more pleasant the experience, the less chance the dog will be defiant. If it becomes this way, it is because you have neglected grooming or are simply too heavy handed.

DOG CRATE

This should be of the size that will accommodate your puppy when it is adult. It will

This Smooth Fox Terrier is chewing on a Nylabone® Gumaknot®. This chew device has been PROVEN safe and effective as a treatment for plaque. No other company's products have the research and history behind them, that's why I recommend Nylabones® over every other dog chew. Owner, Lynne Bockelman.

This Golden Retriever puppy is Starburst's Show 'Em Some Magic. She is owned by Karen Taylor and is being restrained in a puppy play pen. Her Gumaball® and Gumabone® are there to keep her from getting bored. These toys are often referred to as pooch pacifiers.

be useful to effect housebreaking when it is a pup. It will also double as a carry crate when the dog must be transported anywhere and can make a useful bed for the pup while it is a toddler (suitably lined with blankets). Be very sure the crate is large enough for the puppy. So many times I have seen pups and adults in crates that were

Puppies and adult dogs need to chew, play and clean their teeth with jaw exercise devices. A Nylabone® Gumaring® is being enjoyed by this Labrador Retriever. Owner, Sharon Celentano.

This dog crate has many uses. You can ship your puppy in it; your puppy can sleep in it and it helps in training your puppy. Since this Rottweiler puppy will grow quite large, the crate shown will soon be too small. Owner, George S. Chamberlin.

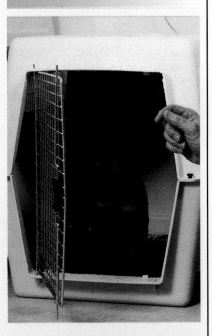

far too small for them. This is cruel. The pup or the adult must be able to stand up without its head or ears touching the roof. It should be able to turn around without touching the sides, and it should be able to lay in a stretched position.

PUPPY PLAY PEN

These are really handy to have both for housebreaking the pup and for placing it in a safe place while you are attending to jobs that do not allow you to keep an eye on your new baby. You can fashion these yourself or purchase them from pet-supply houses or large pet shops. Again, try to obtain one that is as large as you can devote space to.

DOG GATE

These can be purchased in a range of sizes, or the handyperson could easily make his own. They enable you to place the puppy in a given room without the need to close it in such that it cannot see you. Maybe you have a non-fenced yard, so it can be fitted to the kitchen or patio door. You may be eating at the dining table, so can place it on a door that prevents the puppy entering the room to begin its "begging" behavior. Commercial units usually have a spring-loaded mechanism so they are easily fitted to most standard-size door frames.

This lovely Labrador Retriever puppy is relieving his doggie tensions and cleaning his teeth at the same time with this Gumabone® with dental tips. Safe toys are a necessity for puppies and grown dogs. Dogs need to chew! Owner, Diane Ammerman.

TOYS

Take care in your choice of toys for two reasons. One concerns health, the other revolves around their effecting behavior patterns. Cheap plastic toys should be avoided. They are easily torn apart by a puppy and bits could be swallowed with potentially fatal results. Hard rubber balls or dumbbells are acceptable but not nearly as good as Nylabone® and Gumabone®. These hard nylon bones and polyurethane bones come in about 100 sizes and shapes, fitting any size breed, adult or puppy.

COLLARS

Collars come in two basic types. There are the buckle-type ones and the choke chains. Both may be made in leather, nylon, or steel. You will need both a buckle collar and a choke chain for training. A rule you should never forget is that a choke chain should never be left on your puppy or dog when you are not with it. There is always the risk, by the very fact that it is loose fitting, that it may get caught onto something at which the dog will panic and could be injured, or even choke to death.

Leather collars are recommended for daily wear, and those which are round will not as badly damage the neck fur as will flat ones. However, certain breeds, such as Bulldogs, Bull Terriers and mastiff types, traditionally wear wide collars often studded with brass or polished metal

Your pet shop will have many products to show you for assisting your puppy in working off his tensions. Ask him about safety, not about price. The most popular chews are rawhides, but not all are the same quality. The best ones are melted and then molded so they are a unified mass and in the shape of the familiar Nylabone®. The puppy shown here is a Border Collie. Owner, Jerri A. Carter.

embellishments. Initially, you only need purchase an inexpensive neck collar for the puppy as it will soon grow out of this. When it comes to its adult collar, be sure to invest in one which is sewn together rather than held by rivets. The latter often snap at the most inopportune moments. Their "D" ring will also likely be cheap and weak (unsoldered), thus likely to break open under any strain on the lead.

Choke collars may be single or double. The latter may be single stranded or multiple stranded. They are in effect two chains threaded together. The single choke is the most popular and may be a row of metal rings with round or flattened surfaces. At each end it has a welded ring. The alternative is the spiked or pronged choke. This looks rather formidable but is arguably better than the regular choke, especially for the medium to large breeds. It gets results quicker and they tend to be longer lasting. However, it must be of the double-choke type, not one of the old-fashioned single-pronged chokes. The former have a definite "choke" maximum, which is one of the benefits of the double choke. The single choke has a progressive action and could literally choke a dog to death, which cannot happen with a correctly fitting double choke of any type.

Chokes come in a range of lengths and link sizes, so you should select the one appropriate to your breed. In order to gauge the length, measure the puppy's neck

and add about three inches. This will also be how to determine the length needed for the pup when it becomes adult: it will need four inches of slack. As the pup grows, there will be less slack. When you have less than two inches is the time to purchase a longer choke chain.

The correct way to fit the choke to the puppy is as follows: Form the loop with the chain. Now place your hand through this as though this were the pup's neck.

For more advanced training, fully retractable leads are available in different sizes, strengths and lengths to allow owners to match the lead to the size of the dog. Photo courtesy of Flexi USA, Inc.

The ring from the chain that is passing across the *top* of your wrist is the one that the lead will be attached to. If this part of the chain is passing under the puppy's neck, the choke action will not work correctly: it may not loosen up as the puppy stops pulling, nor will it work effectively as a progressive choke.

THE HARNESS

If you have a very small breed of dog, you might wish

to use a harness rather than a regular collar. If you plan to do advanced obedience work and tracking, a harness will of course be a necessity. For small dogs the advantage of the harness is that the puppy or dog cannot wriggle out of this as it might with a collar. Harnesses come in a range of sizes and materials, as well as in styles. As with collars, be sure it is well made and featuring sewn joints rather than rivets. It must also be a snug fit so that it does not chaff and

cause sores to the dog. You cannot train your puppy on a harness, so you still need a buckle collar or choke for this purpose.

LEADS

Leads are available in leather, webbing, and nylon. They may be flat or round, and of course come in a range of lengths. You can also purchase choke leads, with single or double choke. The ideal length for training purposes would be 6 feet. If

These dogs didn't take their master's bed, they took the kid's play bed and called it their own because it had the master's scent.

reason. The lead must be long enough to be held in your right hand—the left hand is then free to either encourage your dog to move alongside you, or to take up the slack for correction purposes if this is needed.

DOG BEDS

If you do not want your puppy, and the adult it becomes, to sleep on your bed or your furniture, you should provide it with its own bed. This should be sturdy and of a size that allows it to recline. It should be placed in a non-drafty position that provides it with seclusion when this is required by it. It can be lined with blankets. There are now a range of good washable blankets, and some of imitation wool, specially made for dogs.

Because puppies will tend to chew on wooden or wicker-type beds, you should consider a fiberglass bed, which are perhaps the best because they do not provide a haven for parasites and are easily cleaned. If you have purchased a large dog crate, this will make a good bed for the puppy. If the pup has come directly from a breeder's litter, you should take a toy and a blanket from the litter so the pup still smells its mom and littermates in his new home. Any good breeder will be happy to accommodate this request.

you plan to do somewhat more advanced training, a long line lead is suggested—one with a length of at least 20 feet. As with the collar, choose only from those which are sewn not riveted together at the handle and clasp ends. The clasp itself should be a strong metal trigger or sprung billet hook and never one made from a thin piece of shaped metal. The latter sort will soon snap open with any but the smallest of dogs on them.

Although you will see a number of short-length stout leads made for the larger dog, I do not recommend these. Their length means they can only be held in the left hand (of a right-handed person) and this places you at a disadvantage should the dog decide to pull for any

Pet shops have a wide variety of dog beds to match your home's decor. This Shih Tzu would probably be happy in any comfortable bed. Owners, John and Prudence Timney.

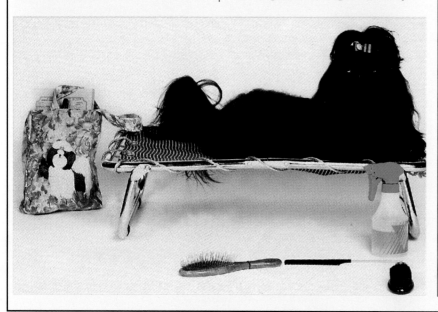

When you own a dog, you own responsibilities. Clipping the nails, grooming the coat, bathing, protecting, training and maintaining health are just a few of the responsibilities which come with dog ownership. But it's worth it when you measure the love and affection you get in return. Whoever said, "A man's best friend is his dog," sure knew what he was talking about. This Dachshund is getting its nails clipped. Owner, Kaye Ladd.

PUPPY ARRIVES HOME

As a rule, collect the puppy as early in the day as possible so that the pup has plenty of time to settle into its new home before bedtime. If you have a long journey to make, advise the seller what time you expect to arrive. Nothing is worse for a puppy than to have been given a meal and then to be placed into a moving vehicle for the first time. This is a recipe for carsickness, and immediately sets a precedent in the pup's mind that travel in cars is not a pleasurable experience.

It is always best that two people are in the vehicle if possible, the second person being responsible for looking after the puppy. If you have purchased a travel crate, this will be its first use. Line it with several layers of paper so that if the puppy should be sick or relieve itself, you are prepared. Have a damp cloth in a plastic bag and an old towel so that the puppy can be cleaned if need be. Take a small quantity of puppy chow with you, a supply of fresh water, and the appropriate bowls for these. If you do not have a dog crate, you can soon fashion a bed for the puppy from a strong cardboard box.

Be sure the vehicle is neither too hot nor cold, and on no account should you visit friends to show them the puppy on your way home. Apart from the fact that its vaccinations will probably not be fully operative as yet, the less it is exposed to potential pathogens (disease-causing

organisms), the better.

You may need to make one or more stops on the homeward journey. If so choose a quiet location well off the road where the puppy can be allowed out of the vehicle, duly supervised, for a few minutes' relief from the vehicle. Do not put it on the ground where there is evidence that other dogs have fouled, and try to avoid contact with other people at this time. The puppy may

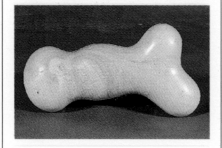

THE GALILEO® is probably the toughest nylon product made for dogs. In three sizes, the Galileo® is for strong chewers and can last for years of chewing, teeth cleaning and jaw massage.

wish to relieve itself.

During the journey your helper can nurse and fuss the puppy, but try to encourage it to have a nap. If children are present, do not let them maul the puppy nor overtax its energy by playing for long periods. It needs a lot of sleep just like all babies do.

ON ARRIVAL HOME

The first thing you should do when you arrive home is to let

ROAR-HIDE™ is the healthiest and safest form of dog treat. It is 100% unbleached rawhide (water buffalo) which has been ground into small pieces and melted. The molten rawhide is then injection molded into the typical Nylabone® shapes.

NYLAFLOSS® is a very useful product. It can last for years and serves as a bonding toy where the master plays tug with the puppy. At the same time, the nylon threads are pulled through the puppy's teeth acting like a dental floss (which it really is). Be sure that you buy the one made of nylon; cotton tugs are too easily destroyed and soiled.

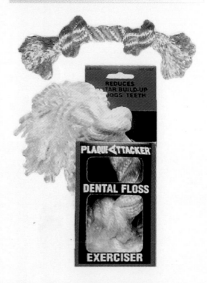

When the puppy arrives at home, you must introduce it to the children. The children must be taught their responsibility to the puppy. This beautiful Shar-Pei has formed an immediate bond with the youngster. Owners, David Melvard and Katherine Fudge.

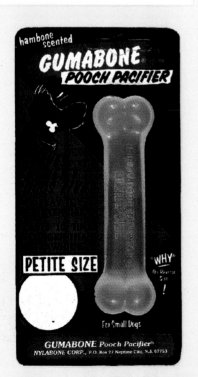

Above: NYLABONE® is the standard of the dog chew industry. It has been on the market for about 40 years and is probably the only nylon dog chew made of VIRGIN nylon. It comes in many sizes and has a proven record of longevity and safety for dogs and many other laboratory animals.

the puppy "spend a penny" in your yard. Carry it to the place you have determined for this purpose. Stand with it and if it urinates or defecates, give it lots of fuss. If you live in an apartment, maybe you have a patio that will be its toilet area, in which case take it to this and place it on a few sheets of newspaper spread on the floor. Alternatively, spread such sheets on your kitchen floor. Once it has attended to its needs, it will no doubt appreciate a little meal and a drink of water or diluted milk.

How Safe Is Your Home?

Your home may contain many potentially dangerous problems for a little puppy not yet wise to the ways of the world:

1. Be sure that there is the minimum of trailing electrical wires around any given room. If these are plugged into live sockets, be aware that puppies have a penchant for trying to chew most things that look remotely edible. If they do not chew on it, they may well tug on it. This could bring a heavy lamp crashing onto the puppy, so inspect each room for such not so obvious dangers. A trailing cord from an iron is especially dangerous to a puppy, so never leave an iron on a board, even for a moment, when a puppy is about.

2. Be sure that all balconies

GUMABONE® is the standard for the soft bone dog chew. It MUST have dental tips and must be made of virgin polyurethane or it is too soft and easily chewed up. Every pet shop sells Gumabone®.

Kids love puppies and puppies love children. Can you see a better example of a Samoyed pup and her mistress?

are suitably screened so the puppy is in no danger at all. Likewise, garden ponds and swimming pools should be screened while your pet is a baby and at risk of falling in. Alternatively, erect a temporary fence that prevents the pup from reaching these areas.

3. Potentially poisonous indoor plants must be placed out of reach of your puppy. Apart from the health risk to the pup, you will not want such plants or other plants to be destroyed by your new companion.

4. Always be aware of drafts created when doors and windows are open. Place a heavy stop against doors so there is no risk these could suddenly slam shut on your puppy.

5. When you are working in the kitchen and likely to be handling boiling pans and their like, be sure the puppy is not present. This

This prize-winning photo of TRUE LOVE was taken by the outstanding dog photographer, Isabelle Francais. Shetland Sheepdog owned by Karen R. Powles.

Your puppy has feelings, just like you or your child. This Chinese Crested puppy seems to have an excellent relationship with its mistress. Owner, Arlene Butterklee.

is where a dog gate will come in very handy.

6. If you have an unfenced yard, then you should consider fencing. Is it possible to construct a dog run before the puppy grows up? Placing the dog on a yard chain is not a satisfactory answer. A yard chain, should it ever be needed at all, is a temporary means of canine confinement. Sadly, one sees all too often poor dogs that are left on these bestial pieces of metal for most of their lives. And their owners often have the nerve to call themselves dog lovers!

PUPPIES AND CHILDREN

Kids just love puppies, and puppies love children. However, as neither can apply any sort of reason to their relationship, it is crucial that you monitor their interactions otherwise you may have a disaster just waiting to happen. Every year thousands of children are mutilated by their own pets. Every year as many puppies are badly injured or killed by children whose parents could not be bothered to either watch over them, or teach them how to respect their pets.

Children may pull at a puppy causing it severe pain; they may lift it up in a painful manner; they may drag it around the home on a piece of string; or place elastic bands around its neck. It is no surprise when a badly treated puppy suddenly, as it gets older, turns around and attacks the child. Some dogs are extremely benign and will accept an unbelievable amount of mauling by

toddlers—others may give them very short shrift and promptly administer their own form of discipline if the owner fails to do so.

If you are not a considerate owner, the chances are neither will your children be. What they see you do they will probably do as well. Never leave a toddler with a large dog, because even if the dog is totally dependable, it can injure a small child just by playing with it.

Always try to appreciate that your puppy has feelings just as you have. Give it plenty of fuss so that it will

Puppies love anything that moves, particularly when it twitters and tweets too. Acclimating the new pup to the family caged bird should be done with care. The pup may never be fully trustworthy with such a tempting little friend.

never become jealous of other family members. A not unfamiliar scenario is when a pup initially becomes a family member it gets lots of fuss. Then the novelty of the pup wears off as it matures and it

All dogs are natural hunters. But if your German Shepherd and pet ferret are introduced in the same household by their mutual master, the chances are good that they can get along, though they'll never be completely trustworthy.

is ignored. Other pets, and maybe human babies, then arrive and the dog is all but forgotten. The dog quite naturally resents the newcomer who is regarded as an interloper. It is challenging its position within the pack, and such a challenge may not go unanswered, depending on the nature of the dog. That is when problems start and manifest themselves by the dog's growling and warning the new pet, by its being more disobedient with the owner, or by other undesirable behaviors.

DOGS AND OTHER PETS

Puppies have an instinctive predisposition to chase things. It is a very low threshold because dogs are prime carnivores (flesh eaters). However, when a puppy sees a kitten, or a rabbit, or even a bird, it is not old enough to know that these other animals would be its dinner in the wild. When your puppy first sees other pets, its reaction is to want to inspect these and then, if they are friendly, to play with them. Out of play the hunting instinct is developed in the wild, but it can be controlled under domestic conditions.

The puppy can be imprinted on other pets so it regards them as other pack members, rather than as a meal. This is why you will see puppies and cats, or rabbits, or other animals, getting along so well together. Always bear in mind that you cannot force a friendship between animals, even of the same species, no more than you can between people. If two animals choose not to be friends, the worst probable situation is that they will tolerate each other, providing they come to realize that the other pet is no physical threat.

If you have a cat, its initial reaction will either be to run, or it will inspect the puppy then promptly hiss at and maybe box its ears before departing. What you must *never* do is to hold the puppy in front of the cat. This could result in the pup being badly scratched: be very alert to young children who may do just this. Leave the puppy and the cat to sort out their own arrangements, which they will do over a few days or a week. Your role is purely supervisory. If a puppy is introduced to a home with a kitten in it, the chances are much better that the two will become friends.

STARTING OUT RIGHT

Training should begin the minute the puppy enters your home. Its behavior patterns do not start a few days or weeks later, after it has settled in, they start in the present. It is altogether easier to prevent bad habits than to correct and cure

Is there anything more beautiful than a puppy and a kitten loving each other? You can enjoy this relationship if you buy them both at a tender age and lead them to believe they are brother and sister.

Your puppy must learn to stay off the furniture. If he doesn't learn this as a puppy, it is very difficult to break him of the habit later on. Owner, Tonee Matteson.

them. It all depends on how you go about things.

Firstly, do not let the puppy wander about the house. If you do, the result will likely be that it will relieve itself on your carpet, and possibly start a bad habit. Restrict the puppy to the kitchen, which is no doubt where it will eat, drink, and be allowed to relieve itself. If you do not want it to get into the habit of sleeping on your chairs and sofa, do not let it go on these in the first place.

You must not punish at all at this time because your objective is to commence the bonding process. If it attempts to clamber onto furniture, simply lift it gently off and say no in a soft voice. Firmness of voice is not needed as yet. If it starts to tug at anything, stop him. It is no use smiling and thinking how cute it is as it hangs on for dear life to your drapes!

You will of course have settled on a short name for the puppy which it needs to know as soon as possible. Use the name constantly—when the pup runs to you give it lots of praise and fuss. If it is doing something you do not want it to do, then move to it as quickly as you can, but without charging such that it frightens the pup.

By all means have a good rough and tumble with it on the carpet. It needs to play and socialize with you as it would in its wild pack situation. Do not of course be too rough with it as it is only a baby animal. When playing with its toys, do not engage in any form of tugging as this merely encourages this pattern of behavior. I know you will see lots of other people doing this with their puppy, but they clearly have not had the benefit of owning this book!

While playing with your puppy, after its initial bursts of energy, and when it is getting a little more subdued, you can place a hand on its chest and your other hand on its rump and gently press the latter so the pup is placed into the sitting position. As you press you can say sit. This is done informally and not in a repetitive manner as with formal training. When the pup is sitting, you can talk soothingly to it and gently stroke its chest. With no problems at all you are already beginning to place in the puppy's mind the association of the word 'sit' with the act of doing this, and you are doing it in a very pleasurable way from the puppy's viewpoint. It is not even aware you have started training already.

MEAL TIMES

It is important that your puppy is fed at regular times. Its food will pass through its digestive system at a given pace. Undigested food will exit at regular intervals. You can work on the basis that your puppy will need to relieve itself within minutes of waking from a sleep, after strenuous play or exercise, and a short

You can't rely on toys alone to make your puppy happy. Puppies need company as they are pack animals and do not enjoy a sole existence.

For no-mess feeding, a feeding tray is very practical. Feeding trays are available in different styles and colors at your local pet shop. Photo courtesy of Penn Plax.

while after it has eaten or drunk. If the meals are irregular, then so will be its potty pattern.

THE FIRST NIGHT

Depending on what sleeping arrangements you have determined for puppy will in turn determine just how much of a problem you have on the first night. If the puppy is to sleep with you on your bed, then there will be no problems. You will provide the warmth and sense of well being that it had with its mother and siblings. On the other hand, if the puppy is to sleep in the kitchen in its crate, you could be in for some howling and whimpering. Quite naturally, it will miss its mother and feel very lonely.

Pet shops have a wonderful selection of dog beds, especially those made by Jim Elesh. Always get a bed larger than you think is comfortable for your puppy . . . puppies grow, you know! This Labrador Retriever will reach 75 pounds!

The best way to prepare for the first night is to place the puppy in its bedding area for short periods during the day. Do this after it has been playing and become tired, thus ready for a nap. You might also leave a radio on softly in the room as this too will have a soothing effect (and so you don't have to hear the whining at night!). If this is done once or twice during the day, the first night might not be as bad as it otherwise could be. You might leave a dim light on when the puppy is put to bed as this will also provide some reassurance for it. Give it the blanket from its litter or a plaything that smells like its siblings.

However, the chances are that the puppy will wake up in the night and start whimpering to a greater or lesser degree. If you go to it when this happens, you will encourage the same behavior again and again. You must therefore ignore its howling in the pup's best interests. On no account should you rush into the puppy and shout at it or spank it, this might discourage it for a while, but you don't want to threaten the pup on its first day! If the howling continues to the extent that you feel your neighbors will also be getting no sleep, then take the pup's crate into your bedroom and this should quiet it, with a few reassuring words.

The next night place the bed back in its selected area and see how things go. Within a few days you should find there are no problems, especially if you repeat the process of letting the pup have naps in its sleeping area during the day. In the winter, give the puppy plenty of warm blankets to cuddle up to.

HOUSEBREAKING YOUR PUPPY

Training your puppy to be clean in its new home is an obvious priority for you. It is not at all a difficult thing to do providing you understand a few simple facts about the entire process of defecation in relation to canines. There are two ways in which a puppy can be taught to attend to its toiletry needs. One is by housebreaking, which by definition means the puppy will go outside to attend these needs. The other is that it can be paper trained so it will relieve itself on paper or, if it is a very small breed, in a litter box.

Some trainers will state that you must choose one or other method from the outset and stick with it because you cannot paper train a puppy on a temporary basis and then expect it to go outdoors later. The claim is that it confuses the puppy. I believe, however, that your puppy has tremendous powers of being able to adjust to new situations providing it understands what is expected of it. You can commence with paper training and progress without any problems to outdoor toiletry habits as long as you go about it in a sensible manner and reinforce the desired action when this is needed.

SCENT MARKING

For the many territorial animals, elimination is more than just the removal from their bodies of unwanted matter but an intrinsic part of their communication system. Scent marking via urine, far more so than fecal deposits, which may often be buried, relays mating signals, signposts, or other trailmarks. Pack members can follow these and thus rejoin their pack should they stray from the path being used.

The scent of your puppy is very unique to it. A dog would never confuse that of one dog with that of another. In the wild the entire territory is scent marked—numerous times in the immediate home range, and less so as this gets further from the actual center of the range. The closer a stray animal gets to the center, the greater the risk it may be seen and attacked.

The significance of this to you as a dog owner is that your puppy has an instinctive desire to scent mark its territory as it matures. This means your house and its immediate surroundings—garden, road and so forth. If the scenting is allowed to happen indiscriminately, it will become extremely difficult for you to keep your house clean as time goes by and your puppy matures. Your object is to have total control over the scent marking so it does not happen inside your home.

PAPER OR LITTER-BOX TRAINING

Whether you paper or litter-box train your puppy is a matter decided upon by

When you see your puppy doing some serious sniffing, you can be sure it's getting ready to urinate. Mature male dogs mark their territories with urine. Sheltie owned by Linda Zimmerman.

yourself, and to some degree determined by the size of your puppy, its sex and breed. Small males, and females up to medium size, can be paper or litter-box trained. Larger breeds of males will need housebreaking, as will females unless you are able to provide a very large litter box for the latter.

The basis of total paper or litter-box training is that the puppy will attend its needs on paper or litter for a brief period or throughout its life, should you so choose. It is a convenient method for owners living in high-rise apartments that do not have immediate access to a yard. It is far less suited to dogs than to bitches because of the former's need to raise its leg and urinate to a high point.

The way to paper train a puppy is to show it the given spot in the home, usually the kitchen, that you want it to relieve itself. Encourage it to relieve itself on newspaper. To train the puppy you must first cover the entire floor with a double layer of newspaper sheets. Praise it whenever doing its business in the right place. Remove the soiled paper, but leave a small amount of urinated paper under a fresh sheet. Move this to the place you wish to be the toilet area. At the same time you can remove one or two sheets from the furthest point from that where the puppy attended its needs, assuming it has used the same spot over two or three days. Use a stain remover on the spot where the puppy first messed.

If you are present when the puppy is about to relieve itself, you can approach it, lift it up gently, and take it to the

Line the floor around the puppy's area with newspapers. The soiled newspapers can then be used again and again to train the puppy to limit its toilet area.

desired spot. Praise it excessively if it does as expected. A puppy wanting to relieve itself will tend to move around the kitchen, sniffing the floor and probably whimpering. It may turn in small circles as well.

If things go as hoped, the puppy will seek out the soiled paper area each time, and as this happens you can steadily make the papered area smaller. If the puppy has clearly not gotten the message, you should *not* punish it but simply go back to the original situation and cover the entire floor and start again. He'll get it the next time.

Try to preempt errors by watching the puppy at the times when it will want to relieve itself in the required area within the first seven to ten days. It is a rather

inconvenient method because it does mean your kitchen must have paper down throughout the period, but in the long run you will be glad you made the effort.

Litter-box training is done in the same manner, but in this instance a litter box is placed in the required location. Whenever the puppy is seen to start attending its needs, it is lifted up and placed into the box. Much praise is given when it does as required. You reduce the paper covering on the floor in the same way as paper training. A small amount of fecal matter can be placed into the box to provide the needed scent for the puppy. By placing the pup in the box after it has played, awoke from sleep, or after eating, it will eventually get the message and oblige you.

The litter box is superior to paper because it is a more natural surface for the puppy and allows it to scratch litter over its fecal matter. There are, however, a couple important points to bear in mind. Firstly, the box must be large enough to accommodate the puppy with ease. Secondly, the sides should not be so high as to make it difficult for the pup to enter the box. The actual material used as litter is not important as long as it is absorbent. You can use cat litter, which comes in various qualities and is the best hygienic choice.

Once you see that the puppy is using the litter tray, it is important that it is kept clean of any fecal matter or urine. Neither dogs nor cats like to walk in a soiled litter box. Problems can often arise because the owners do not clean them after each use.

HOUSEBREAKING

To housebreak your puppy, keep a close watch on it during its first day in the home. Periodically take it to the litter box, and hold in position for just a few seconds. It is given lavish praise. We are always able to spot it at some point when it is ready to relieve itself. If it should mess on the kitchen floor (without your seeing it), clean it immediately, neutralize it, and forget it. We work on the basis that a few errors must be expected.

Once the puppy is using its litter box, and when the vaccination safety period has passed, the puppy is then taken into the outside yard at the times it is likely to want to relieve itself. Now, a puppy cannot control its bowels for very long. If it is taken to a

If you have to leave a young puppy alone for an extended period, it is advisable to add some shredded newspaper to his crate to absorb his urine in case of an accident. This chocolate Labrador Retriever puppy is very content in his "den."

predetermined area on a regular basis, it will use this, and get lavish praise. If it needs to go to the toilet when the kitchen door is closed, it will automatically use its litter box. It has no problem using either if it is encouraged to do

Housebreaking a puppy is most easily done if it is restrained in a small area. Then, when let out, the puppy should be taken to a safe area for it to relieve itself. Owner, George S. Chamberlin.

so. The transition from litter box (or paper) to outside does not happen overnight, but *always* happens over just a few weeks. By preference, a puppy will choose a yard to a litter box or paper every time—it is far more natural for it. After such a period the puppy will cease using its box, providing it is taken out on a regular basis, which all puppies should be. With each passing week, the puppy is a little more able to control its bowels. We also place the litter box right near the kitchen door.

When the door is left open for long periods, the box is

Bring your dog to the same area to relieve himself every time. Dogs like to sniff out their previous landmarks and reinforce them.

placed just outside the door. By this progression there really is no problem, so to say that if you use this or that method you cannot move to another method is misleading. I do not say that we have never owned a "dirty" dog, nor even a cat, but that fact is not related to the manner in which we go about the housebreaking process. Any method is not guaranteed 100% over all dogs, because some dogs simply are not as clean in their habits as others. Generally, females of any species are cleaner than males and are not as preoccupied with scent marking—so it is the males that must be especially watched and trained with greater care.

Any canine can "forget" his housetraining at a future date. Many factors contribute. The dog may not be having the opportunity to relieve itself as it should. It may develop an intestinal problem that prevents it from controlling its bowels. It may become fearful or stressed because of the way it is treated after the novelty of puppy ownership has passed with its owners. Patience and understanding are key in every instance.

CONCLUDING COMMENTS

In closing, bear in mind that certain conditions must prevail in order to ensure your dog's housebreaking success.

1. The puppy must be confined to a given area, preferably one that has an easily cleaned floor, such as the average kitchen. This confinement must be maintained until the puppy is paper or litter-box trained, or housebroken.
2. Do not target the potty area to be close to either food or water dishes. No animal likes to defecate or urinate near its food.
3. The puppy must be fed at regular times so you are able to more readily know when it is likely to want to relieve itself.
4. The puppy must be in good health. If it has diarrhea, it will clearly be unable to control its bowels for even a few moments and will make errors.
5. The puppy must be exercised at least three times *every* day. This provides the needed opportunity for it to relieve itself.
6. Once the puppy is housetrained, you must respond promptly to it when it indicates it wishes to go outside. If you ignore its pleas because you are doing something else, you are forcing the dog to relieve itself in your home.
7. You must *always* praise success.
8. Try to avoid the temptation of reprimanding your pet if you see it going to a spot that is other than where it should go. If you do ever reach the point where a no is justifiable, you must catch the puppy in the act. Then take it to the right spot, place it down, and give praise.

Most of all try to use your logic and understanding of what is happening in the puppy's mind in relation to what you now know about scent marking.

Finally, remember that in some areas you are legally responsible for picking up after your dog. Even if not required by law, you should regard this as a social responsibility. Purchase a pooper-scooper or similar tool from your pet shop and be a responsible dog owner. It would also be wise, from a health viewpoint, to regularly remove and dispose of fecal matter from your yard and garden.

Many dogs sniff out an area to find a suitable spot to relieve themselves. If a dog comes across an area previous marked by another male dog, it might hesitate, as shown by this puppy, or just ignore the scent and do its stuff!

KINDERGARTEN TRAINING

The most important commands your puppy must understand and obey are **sit, stay, down, heel, and come.** With these well performed your puppy will take its place as a model little canine citizen in society. Regardless of whether you plan to train your dog to the gun, to compete in field trials, advanced obedience tests, tracking, or learning party tricks, it must first learn these basic commands.

Before we begin training, let's keep in mind:

1. Never undertake any formal training lesson if you are not in a good mood. If you do not adhere to this rule, you will almost certainly lose your patience with your puppy. This can only result in frustration and problems for you both.
2. Never make lessons long and boring. Restrict the early sessions to no more than ten minutes each. You can, however, give the puppy three or four lessons over the course of a day.
3. Always commence and end lessons on an upbeat. This means start with something the puppy can already do. Give praise. This will set the pattern for what is to follow. End with something the pup can do so that its memory of lessons is pleasurable.
4. Spend a few minutes playing with the puppy after a lesson. This again acts as a reinforcer that lessons are fun.
5. If things are not going well, do not continue with the lesson. End with something positive. Your puppy will only learn from what it does right, not from what it does wrong.
6. Never physically punish your puppy if it is doing badly—this will only reinforce the notion that training sessions are not pleasurable. If the pup is not doing well, it simply does not know what is expected of it.
7. Always keep commands short. If you start to yell out long sentences, these are meaningless and will merely frustrate the puppy.
8. Make notes on problem areas so these can be studied when you have time to sit and think things out. The problem is almost certainly of your making rather than of the puppy's. Remember, you are the teacher, not the puppy.
9. Always conduct training sessions where there are no other distractions— which includes other people. You need to get your puppy's full concentration. Pups can only concentrate for a few minutes at a time, after which their mind will start to wander to other things. That is the way with all juvenile animals, so never expect your puppy to be different.

Training is important. Wouldn't you look silly having a tug-of-war every time you took your puppy out for a walk! This Bearded Collie has a mind of its own! Owner, Penny Hanigan.

10. Never attempt to teach a given command within a certain number of lessons. It is not important that your puppy progresses as rapidly as a neighbor's pup or one owned by a friend. Other pups may be more intelligent than yours, their owner may have a greater talent to train than you have, or it may be a mixture of these reasons. If you are satisfied that progress is being made, then things will work out, even if it takes a little longer than you perhaps anticipated.

If things just are going from bad to worse, then you must stand back and reevaluate what might be going wrong. Normally, the best course to take is to go right back to the beginning and start again.

TRAINING IS A CONTINUUM

Believe it or not, your puppy is quite capable of learning a number of things concurrently with each other. It may grasp one command readily, while another takes longer. Formal training sessions may start at a given time, but prior to this you can begin teaching the puppy in an informal manner—a sort of kindergarten period when there are no negatives in the form of verbal or any other forms of discipline or correction. This prepares the puppy for formal lessons and makes these much easier.

PRE-FORMAL TRAINING

During the first few days after you have brought your little puppy home, you will of

Retriever training is easy, especially if you use a scented Frisbee® made especially for dogs (note the bone molded into the top). Retrieving is not kindergarten training, but it can be taught at an early age, especially if your dog has a natural talent for chasing. Dalmatian puppy owned by Darlene Woz.

course be commencing with its paper or housebreaking training. During this time you will also be able to teach it the come command by calling its name. You can add come after using its name. Use an excited voice and bend down or kneel so that the puppy is better able to focus on you. When it reaches you, give it lots of fuss and say "good boy or girl."

After fussing with it a few moments, you can then gently place it in the sit position by holding one hand to its chest and using the other to press down its rump. At the same time say sit and, once the puppy is in the sit position, you again lavish praise on it for a job well done. Do not repeat this

immediately because the object is to do this preschool type work in a very casual manner. It is essentially part of the come command that is being learned, also in a very laid-back manner. Be sure you do not make this into a formalized ritual.

Within the first two days you can place a collar onto the puppy and at that time have a game with the pup. The idea is to let the puppy become familiar with the feel of a collar. You can take it off after about an hour and then put it back on later. It will initially scratch at the collar, which is why this is the time to distract it by playing. Very quickly the collar will be forgotten.

Next time attach a lead to the collar and let the puppy

trail this behind it for a few moments at a time. If it starts to mouth and bite the lead, call the pup to you and play with it or remove the lead. You do not want it to get into the habit of biting at the lead. If the puppy starts to jump up at you, which most will, the best thing to do is to gently take its front paws and place them back on terra firma, then play with it. Say no in a soft voice as you grasp its paws. Once again you are discouraging a pattern before it

You cannot spoil a puppy as long as it is well trained. The fancy bed, stuffed animal and alpha-blocks are not necessary but are part of the fun of having a puppy, provided the puppy doesn't start chewing on these basically unsafe toys.

can begin to form—that of jumping up at you. Once the puppy is familiar with having a lead attached to its collar, you can next take hold of the lead and allow the puppy to walk around the room as it desires. Every so often you can gently let the lead become taut so the puppy gets its first impression of restraint. When this happens the puppy will

probably pull back against the lead and commence a bronco-type performance. However, the minute this happens make sure the lead goes limp and call the puppy to you. This distracts its attention from what was happening. Let it then carry on walking around.

Your objective is to allow the puppy to gradually become familiar with the tension on the lead. If you go about this in the right way, you will find that within just a few days you can coax the puppy to go where you want, rather than the other way around. There will be progressively fewer and fewer objections. Always encourage the puppy to follow you—if needs be, by offering it a tasty tidbit. However, try not to rely too much on treats in any aspect of training. Rather, let your fuss and praise be the main reinforcer of a behavior pattern as this is far more reliable in the long haul.

WHEN TO COMMENCE FORMAL TRAINING

One of the greatest errors many people make is to

You cannot train two puppies at one time. It is too difficult to keep their attention. Training must be individualized for each dog, always a one person-one dog situation.

commence formal training sessions too early in the puppy's life. These should not start until the pup is about four months old. A puppy should be given the time to mature so that

If it is your intention to have more than one puppy, training becomes twice the chore. These puppies have been trained to STAY and they are watching and listening to their master/ mistress for further commands.

The Pug and the child might have a problem as to the ownership of the alpha-block toy. Though it is not serious to the adult, it could be a serious problem between the puppy/child relationship.

it is physically and mentally capable of coping with any advanced form of training. We live in an age when it seems too many people want to achieve their goals too early.

Formal lessons are those where you will devote a set amount of time to training per se, rather than by the casual methods outlined as being kindergarten training. Up until the four-month mark, you will rely largely on stopping the puppy from doing unwanted things by removing it from them and by using the word no with a soft tone to your voice. Once training proper is commenced you will start to put more bite into the word. Do not do this suddenly just because the puppy has had its four-month birthday, but rather on a build-up basis.

The kindergarten period is as important for you as it is for the puppy. It gives you time to ponder exactly what training is all about. You are able to learn about your own shortcomings at this time, how to be patient, and how not to try to correct a puppy for something that was done minutes before.

Until this puppy was four months old he was trained in DON'T DO THAT; after this stage it is time for the DO THIS program. This willing and able Doberman puppy is owned by Carol Kepler.

SIT, STAY AND DOWN COMMANDS

In teaching your puppy to learn these three commands, you can introduce hand signals, and even a whistle for one of them. The advantage of hand signals is that they may be useful when the dog is out of hearing range but can still see you. The whistle can be of similar benefit as it is very distinctive and can be heard beyond the range of the voice. Select one designed for dogs—then purchase two of them just in case you misplace one.

If you intend to use hand or whistle signals, it is as well to use them from the outset. With regards to whistle signals, decide what these are to be before you start. For example, you may use one long blast to tell the dog to stay, and two or three short blasts to call it to you. For the average pet, these two signals will be all that should be needed. They must be quite distinct otherwise the dog will not know which is which.

With kindergarten over you can now commence with short formal lessons of ten to 15 minutes at first. After about two weeks, you can extend the sessions to about 20 minutes because your puppy should by then be getting quite good if you have had two or three sessions every day. Initially, your object is simply to get the puppy to obey the command. However, as you progress, the pup should become more precise at each command. By this I mean that it will sit correctly and heel precisely,

not simply heel in a somewhat sloppy manner.

To what level of precision your dog should perform will be determined by how high your training goals are. Don't aim too high, but not too low either. If you plan to enter your puppy into obedience trials, then each of the exercises must be trained to a very high standard. But if

Using a favorite Nylabone®, this dog is being trained to HEEL SIT. Photo courtesy of Nylabone, Ltd., England.

your puppy is a pet, and nothing more, then you want it to perform commands in a smart manner without the need to act as though it was on a drill and watching your every move. In an obedience test, you will be expected to make sudden right and left turns, and the dog will be expected to move closely with you all the way. In everyday life you would never walk in the manner of a trainer in a competition ring, so there is no need to be this precise.

SIT

If you have worked on this command during the kindergarten stage, your puppy may well be a proficient sitter by now. If not, then now you must really get down to practicing this exercise. Call the puppy to you and give praise. Now hold one hand on its chest and press down on the rump with the other hand while giving the command sit in a firm voice. There is no need to shout at the puppy because it is not deaf. You should practice saying the word in a firm and authoritative manner without being overbearing. There can be no question at all of the pup's not obeying, because if it gets into its mind that you lack conviction it will certainly try to get away with more and more.

If you say sit and the puppy does not, your reaction is to give no more than a couple of seconds for the pup to think

Children should be encouraged to train their own pets. It is training for both the animal and the child. Owner, Karen S. Powles.

STAY

Place the puppy in the sit position in front of you and say stay. At the same time raise your hand, palm forward. If the puppy gets up and moves toward you, or creeps forward on its butt, lift it up, place it back in the original position, which is important, and say sit followed by stay. Again, when success has been achieved a couple of times, do not push your luck and move on to a different command so that you keep the pup's interest and start to build on a series of rapid short successes. A young puppy may sit in a rather sloppy one-sided manner. I would not worry at this stage. It will correct itself as the puppy matures, and also as it moves on to heel and sit exercises.

Once the pup understands the stay command, you can

This pair loves their training sessions. Training cements a wonderful bond between owner and puppy.

about the command. You then assist it and repeat the command. Do not throw in " be a good boy for mommy or daddy" because this is unneeded at this time. Remember, you are not inviting it to sit but commanding it to do so. This same policy must be adopted with all commands.

If the puppy rolls over when you place it in the sit position, simply lift it to the required position and say sit. What you must guard against is too many repetitions to the degree that the puppy starts to get bored or frustrated. If this looks as though it is becoming the case, get it to do one more sit and then give lots of praise and have a little game. After a few moments, move on to another command exercise before ending that session.

The DOWN command can be either vocal or a hand signal. Both signals can be given at the same time, though only one signal should ever be necessary. Owner, Joelle G. White.

move a few feet further back and repeat this over the next few days—moving steadily further away as the days go by. Do bear in mind that a puppy's powers of concentration are short. Once it has been at the stay for a few seconds, you can use the come command and have the puppy rush to you. At first I would not expect the pup to take up the sit position on the recall, because I want it to get plenty of fuss for the stay. However, as time goes by, you will call it to you and when it reaches you, the sit command will be used so it does this for just a second or two after which it receives praise.

Once the sit, stay and recall have been effected, and the pup reaches you full of joy, do not let it jump up at you. Stand up and bend over to praise it. If it does jump up simply place its front feet back on the floor before you praise it. The puppy always must associate the praise for the right thing. This is why the sit after the recall will be useful because it cannot jump up at you and be sitting.

In the early stages of the stay command, you need not use a whistle signal. Concentrate on the voice and hand signal. Once the pup understands these commands, then is the time to introduce the single blast for the stay, and two or three quick blows for the recall.

DOWN

The down command is a useful exercise for your puppy to learn. However, for the average pet companion I do not regard its inclusion within basic obedience important for the act itself, but rather because it has high value as an obedience exercise from a mental standpoint. The reason is that, to a dog, any form of lying down as a directive is an act of submission. This is why I think all dogs should learn this. More so than the sit, stay, or come, you will find the down command a little more difficult to achieve with any strong-willed dog—so it will test your resolve! There are two basic ways in which the down can be taught. I will discuss these so you can draw your own conclusions as to which is the best for your puppy. Evaluate the good and bad points, relate them to your breed and dog's

disposition, then stick with your plan of action rather than give up and change.

The two methods are 1) using the lead to pull the puppy down and 2) pulling the front legs forward while pressing the shoulders down. In method 1 the lead is passed under your left foot. The right hand holds the lead and the left hand presses at the pup's shoulders. As you say down you press the shoulders and pull on the lead so it forces

This puppy is learning DOWN. All dogs do not have an equal ability to learn; dogs, like people, have different personalities.

the puppy down. Your position for this can be at right angles to the puppy just ahead of its front paws, or with the puppy at your left side. A variation on this is that you have the pup sitting to your left. Now place your left hand, palm down, over the lead near to the collar, while your right hand holds the rest

of the lead. As you say down press firmly with your left hand thus forcing the puppy to the floor.

With method 2 there are also two variations. You can have the puppy to your left and in the sit position. Next, you take both of the puppy's legs at the elbows (or between the elbows and the knee joint) with your right hand. As you say down you gently pull the pup's legs forward, at the same time pressing its shoulders down with your left hand. The second way will be more useful with the larger puppy or young dog. Take hold of the lead near the collar so that it is at the back of the pup's neck. Place your right hand behind the pup's right leg and take hold of its left foot at the knee joint. As you say down you will move the pup's left leg forward. As you do this it will automatically push its right leg forward because at the same time you use your left arm to press on the pup's shoulders. Your right arm will effectively push the pup's right leg forward.

I prefer to use the first variation of method 2 because it takes the path of least resistance. Variation one of this method is normally an option even with the larger puppy. It is less intimidating than the others.

The negatives of method 1 are that the puppy will try its best to resist the downward pull by the lead, and is much more able to do this than when its front feet are simply taken from under it, which requires virtually no effort. From a mechanical viewpoint, a pup's back is able to resist downward pressure, but is of little use in preventing its body going downwards if the paws are not on the ground to use as a lever, which they are not when you use either of the leg pull variations.

There is another aspect that should be taken into account. When using the lead pull method on a large-boned young puppy, the resistance caused by the pup's natural reaction means that unnecessary pressure is being placed onto the knee joints at the very time that this is most inadvisable from a developmental standpoint. Further, the method is not really conducive to the whole concept of avoiding any aspects of training that are unpleasant for the puppy. Clearly, training as such is unpleasant because it involves discipline, but the less of this that can be used, the better. You must repeat this command a number of times until the puppy is able to register in its mind what you want. Once it has succeeded two or three times the session should be ended on a high note. You must practice the down each day until the pup is proficient. Only then can you start using the down and stay command. This is taught in the same manner as the sit and stay.

Once the puppy will sit and down from a distance of a few yards, you can then polish off the exercise by having the pup sit, down, and sit before a recall. But remember do not bore the pup to death with unneeded repetitions of the sit and down. It is altogether better to do these over a longer period than to try and cram them into a few days, which will tend to become a real chore to your puppy. It is also better to move onto other exercises so

the sessions contain a number of things for the puppy to think about. Its "repertoire" will thus be made up of some commands it has mastered and others which it's only beginning to master.

Some trainers do not take this view and feel that dogs should be drilled until they are perfect at each command before progressing to the next. This really is boring for both

This Akita demonstrates the DOWN/STAY. The owner is Gloria Jean Richardson. The dog is Kiri Yama Bijin Eiko Suzuki CGC. She has earned the Canine Good Citizen title from the American Kennel Club, which means she is proficient in all basic obedience commands.

puppy and owner. It implies that the pup can only cope with one exercise at a time and this is not true. The more varied the tasks being worked at any one moment, the more interesting everything becomes.

The hand signal that is used

for the down is to hold your arm upwards, palm facing the puppy, then bring it down in one single sweeping movement. Do not wave your hand up and down like a piston, but repeat the exercise many times over a number of days and it will eventually register.

How Long to Teach These Commands?

Very often beginners want to have some idea as to how long it should take for their puppy to learn the basic commands. This is difficult to answer because so much depends on the individuality of the puppy, the patience of the trainer, and indeed the breed of puppy being taught. Even so I will venture a few guidelines—but I stress they should not be used as a specific timeframe for basing the training program on. If you are working with your puppy twice a day, then it should be quite possible for the pup to learn these exercises inside one week, and become quite proficient at them within two weeks. While I am a great believer in not pushing things, we must distinguish between how long is a reasonable amount of time for a simple command to be registered in a dog's mind. If a puppy is not showing good response within a few sessions, then this clearly indicates that the trainer is going wrong somewhere.

The most common problem is that a pet owner will not commit to a regular training schedule, or that he starts to take a wishy-washy attitude to his dog's protest at being unwilling to sit or take up the down position, etc. Once you are satisfied that your puppy understands a command, then failure to do the exercise means it is being disobedient. This must of course be treated appropriately otherwise your puppy will start to disobey more and more of your instructions. If the pup understands the sit command, but takes its time to do it, your authority must be asserted. Stand with the pup at your left side and say sit in a much firmer voice. If the command is not obeyed promptly, hold the pup by the collar, press its rump down and give the command with more bite in your voice. Once a command is understood, it should not be allowed to regress or be ignored. Remember if you are not prepared to insist that a command is obeyed, do not give the command in the first place.

This Maltese puppy is literally in the hands of the owner. The puppy can be a well-disciplined house mate or a difficult companion because it could be untrained, not housebroken and prone to crying. The training you give your puppy will last a lifetime. Owner, Robin Lindemann.

THE HEEL COMMAND

The heel command is very obviously a crucial need for your puppy to understand well—the more so the larger the breed you have. Nothing is more frustrating than to be taken for a walk at high speed by your dog! Some owners, amazingly, accept this situation and endure it for years, when for a little effort they could have enjoyed their walk with Rover. Other owners steadily reduce the number of times they take their pets out. This is very much a backward step as far as dog ownership goes.

Yet other owners take the view that since they only have a small dog it takes no effort to hold it in check at the end of its lead. What they overlook is the fact that if a little dog suddenly moves to the side when the lead is at full length it could easily trip someone. You must therefore determine that, come what may, your puppy will be taught to walk correctly on its lead.

Walking to heel is not a natural action for a dog, and even less so for a puppy. It is often the most difficult command for the average pet owner to accomplish (which is why so many give up on it). It is specifically for this reason that I have discussed other basic commands first. If the sit, stay and down commands are well understood by the puppy before heel work begins, they will actually make heel work somewhat easier. This is because the puppy is beginning

to accept mild corrective training. This will be taken a step further with heel work.

Also, the previous exercises can all be done within the confines of your home, but for heel work, you will need to go outside, unless you have a very long passage in your home. Even then, I would advise you to practice these exercises outdoors because the puppy always enjoys going out.

THE TARGET OBJECTIVE

Your objective with heel work is to end up in a situation where your puppy will walk by your left side (or right if you are left handed) without pulling ahead nor lagging behind. If you make a change of direction, your puppy will move with you. It will not be a number of feet away from your left side but will walk no more than about 9 inches from your leg, and with its head level with your knee. If you plan to enter obedience competitions, it will need to be even closer to you. However, this level of precision is not vital for a companion dog. Indeed, I would not want a dog walking so close to me that its head was virtually resting on my knee!

However, when you come to a stand-still, you want your dog very close by your side so it all but touches you. With an average-sized adult this will mean that you could scratch the back of its ears without having to reach forwards, backwards, or sideways. If so, the dog is in the correct heel

position. Your second objective with heel work is that when you come to a stand-still the puppy will sit down automatically.

HEEL WORK REQUIREMENTS

For heel work you will need a 6-foot lead, a collar, and a choke chain. Ideally, you should commence against a wall or similar structure where the pup's lateral movements are restricted. This will mean you only have to concern yourself with the pup's tendency to want to move ahead of you (most likely) or lag behind you if it lacks confidence in you or itself.

When doing heel work, the way in which you have gone about bonding and taught your puppy the other basic commands will have considerable bearing on how well the puppy will heel. If you have been overbearing, the chances are that the puppy will be fearful of you. As such it will definitely not want to walk too close to you. This will mean you will need to apply more lead corrections, and this will obviously make the puppy even more fearful of you.

All too often you can see dogs that are being pulled, jerked and yelled at by their owners. The poor little souls are terrified and simply cannot understand what they are supposed to do. The owners expect them to understand exactly why they are being moved from an environment they have never previously left, and to do things they have never previously had to do.

If you have attended to kindergarten work, this will make life altogether easier because the puppy will already be familiar with its collar, lead, and maybe even its choke chain. It should know what restraint feels like. If you did not attend to this preparatory work, regardless of the age of the puppy, I would suggest you do so before you venture outside to commence heel training.

LEAD CORRECTIONS

The term lead correction means using the lead to communicate to the puppy that it is doing something wrong. You do not hit the puppy with the lead but use a jerking action to correct a puppy from moving ahead or to the side. If a puppy lags behind, I would not use a lead correction because this will not remedy what is clearly a matter of fear or lack of confidence. This, hopefully, will be overcome by encouragement. When using the lead correction, you must assess the degree of severity that is needed with your particular puppy. With a timid or small breed, you will not need to jerk the lead as hard as with a larger, more aggressive or head-strong breed. The dog need not be large to be difficult and obstinate.

Certain bull and terrier breeds have a higher pain threshold, meaning that it will take more discipline to persuade them to obey than it would for other comparably sized, or even larger, breeds. Some people confuse what they term stupidity with pain

thresholds or strong instincts. A breed may appear stupid because it resists training, but this does not make it a stupid dog. A Staffordshire Bull Terrier, for example, *may* be extremely difficult to train in certain aspects, such as heel work, especially if it sees another dog while out walking.

A German Wirehaired Pointer at HEEL. The dog is Schnellberg's Reba Jean CDX owned by Barbara Skurya.

However, it may be otherwise a very intelligent dog that can open a drawer to get its collar and lead when being taken out. It may even learn all of the usual little tricks such as handshaking, begging, rolling over and so on with no difficulty whatsoever. A

breed's natural tendencies can always affect its trainability.

So, before you begin any training exercises always try to take account of these breed characteristics, because these really do influence how well a dog will respond not only to given commands but also to the situation.

MAKING A START

I will assume you have found a wall to walk against with your puppy. Hold the lead in your right hand, which will leave your left hand free to jerk or relax the lead as needs dictate. Even when trained, you should always walk your dog holding the lead in your right hand. This is because, and especially so with a powerful dog, it enables you to reel in the dog should it suddenly pull forward. If it did this when you were holding the lead with the left hand, as you will see many people do, it could easily take you off balance.

When you commence heel training, you should do so with the puppy at your left side and in the sit position. You then begin to walk and at the same time you can say Rover, heel. At first the puppy's inclinations are to bound off ahead of you, so it is a good idea to take up some of the slack so that the pup cannot actually move too far ahead before you jerk on the lead with your left hand. As you do this, you say heel.

It may take a few corrections before the puppy begins to get the message. If it persists in pulling, you should increase the severity of the jerk, and the tone of your voice when giving the command. Keep the first two lessons short, maybe ten minutes or so each. One session in the morning and one in the afternoon is recommended. Once you have traveled the length of the wall, and turned to go back, you will probably have no lateral aid, and the puppy will tend to move further away from you to the left. Do not unduly worry about this in the first few sessions as this will soon be corrected. Once two or maybe three sessions have been completed, or as soon as the pup is responding to corrections, you can try to bring the puppy back to the heel position simply by saying heel in a firm voice. Hopefully this will be sufficient to register in the pup's mind that if the command is ignored the jerk will quickly follow. If the pup still moves ahead, you give a quick jerk on the lead and repeat heel. Some pups seem real smart and grasp the idea very quickly, others seem too preoccupied with moving ahead, so they quickly forget what they are supposed to do.

There are two ways you can help a pup to concentrate. One is to obtain a switch, which is no more than a thin branch from a sapling tree, or a fine cane—the sort you use in the garden to support tall flowers. When this is used, you will hold it in the right hand and tap the pup on the nose the minute it starts to forge ahead. I stress the word tap because the object is simply to remind the puppy not to move ahead of you. In no way should the tap actually hurt or frighten the puppy.

The second option, and the one I prefer, is simply to let out a little more lead. When the pup starts to get ahead, you make a sudden stop and grasp the lead firmly with your left hand. This stops the pup dead in its tracks and may even spin it off balance. Turn around and walk in the opposite direction. Say Rover, heel, once you have started to walk in the opposite direction. You can pat your left knee using you left hand. When the

This Soft Coated Wheaten Terrier is at HEEL. The dog is Casey O'Malley owned by Carol Shaltz.

pup arrives in position, simply say "good boy or girl" and continue with the exercise. Once this has happened two or three times, the puppy will realize that it's best to stay near to you and watch your movements carefully.

The pace you should walk at will again reflect the size of the puppy. Do not make it too fast, but neither should it be too slow. Slow heeling should only be attempted when the puppy is a lot more mature and less impetuous, otherwise it will be one long lead correction.

Once the puppy is walking nicely in relation to its position at your side, you can start to concentrate efforts on bringing it closer to you if it is tending to move too far to the left. At first you will try to encourage it by patting your left leg and saying "good boy" when it stays near to you. You can give a little tug on the lead using your right hand as you pat your knee. If this is not producing results, a more drastic remedy is needed. This is where the slightly longer lead will be useful.

Locate a post of some sort, or a slim tree, and head toward it such that the pup will go on one side while you go on the other. The result will be that the pup will suddenly get a shock when it runs out of lead and you are still walking! Stop when the obvious has happened and, without showing any annoyance, call the dog to heel and praise him when he takes up position.

Now, you may be thinking that this increasing level of unpleasant consequences is a bit hard on your puppy, but always bear in mind the following. Your puppy can learn what is required by receiving much praise and fuss. But you cannot teach it what is not required by this approach. You learned not to miss a nail with a hammer by whacking your thumb. It was not pleasant, but it was an effective teacher. With your puppy you are always commencing by using the most gentle form of discipline you can.

Once a command is understood you can improve it with practice and praise. But sooner or later you may have no option but to let the puppy find out the hard way that if it does not use its own brain to work out the path of least resistance, then it is responsible for the consequence of its own actions. Once a puppy has been pulled up short against a post, it will more quickly want to stay closer to you and avoid this happening in the future—it will start to watch you to make sure nothing will come between it and you. It is using the intelligence it was born with. The same logic applies when you make sudden turns if it is moving ahead.

THE LAGGING-BEHIND PUPPY

For most pups the problem that will need correction is the tendency to want to race ahead. But what if the pup lags behind? There are two methods that will correct this. One is rather harsh, the other is much less so. Which you adopt will depend on how fast you want results, and how you view the way in which an objective is achieved. My own view is that I would always choose the more gentle approach. But I have no qualms at all in raising the discipline level if the softer approach simply is not bringing results. At the end of the day a puppy must be trained, so it is a case that whatever level of discipline is needed must be justified by the long-term benefits it gives to the puppy and the owner.

If a pup is lagging behind and you do not slow down

your pace, the result will be that the pup will tend to sit on its backside and rebel against the lead. However, if you ignore this and press on, the puppy will obviously buck and twist and be dragged along the floor on its butt. This will prevail until it realizes that the only way it can avoid its predicament is to catch up with you and so relieve the tension on the lead. When this decision is made by the puppy, and it may take a little time, it receives praise for coming to heel.

However, while this may hold true for a strong-willed puppy, it may not do so for the ones that are timid. It may result in this particular problem being overcome rapidly, but it may adversely affect the puppy in other ways that may have no connection with heel work. It is an established fact that the only sure thing about stern discipline is that it is totally unpredictable in the way it affects any given individual. With this in mind, I would always take the least severe means of reaching an objective, even though this might take a little longer.

If a puppy lags behind, the first thing that should be done is to gently give short tugs on the lead while calling the puppy to you. I would not, however, go back to the pup but would wait until it decided to come to me—which it should if the come command has been a pleasant learning experience. When a puppy lags behind on a lead, it is usually because it is rebelling against the lead. This can only mean it simply was not given sound kindergarten work before it ever left your home

for its formal training. This can best be resolved by encouragement, but that means using a lot of patience.

If the puppy shows no indication of responding to your soft approach, make life that little bit more uncomfortable for it. Pull it along a little, then encourage it to come to you. This represents the halfway stage between the two extremes.

The beginner's course which I advise is always to take the soft approach but to be prepared to step up the discipline level once a session or two have been completed. Eventually, the puppy will overcome its fear of the lead and accept the restriction this places on it, and will happily walk beside you.

LOCATION PRACTICE

Once your puppy is really coming along well with its heel work, you should practice this every time you take it out. It should not take long at all to see really good results if you insist on the pup's heeling when on the lead. When it first goes out for a walk, this is when it will be excited and want to forge ahead, so this is the time you must make needed corrections.

Just because your puppy will heel well in a quiet locality does not mean it will do so if suddenly taken where it is busy and there are lots of people and other distractions. Try to introduce the pup to different locations on a gradual basis. This will reduce the risk that it will panic and that you will over react by getting short-tempered with the puppy. This of course would only make matters worse.

With the HEEL command under your belt, there are many exercises that you and your puppy can undertake together. This is just the beginning of many possible lessons that will strengthen your bond and make your puppy a happier, obedient member of society.

HEEL-RELATED COMMANDS

With the commands so far covered having been mastered, your puppy is now well on the way to being a well-trained and thus obedient dog. The mere fact that it can perform these exercises means you have established a level of control over it that will be so very useful to you in the day-to-day relationship with your puppy. If the commands are being executed with reasonable precision, you deserve congratulations for a job well done. I am sure you will feel a growing sense of achievement and can feel justifiably proud of the standards so far attained. So why stop at this point?

HEEL AND SIT

This exercise is the easiest of the heel-related commands for your puppy to learn. As you come to a stand-still when walking your puppy, it should sit at your side, close to your left leg. Some trainers insist that the sit is automatic every time you stop. Unless you plan to enter obedience trials or the like, this is not essential. As such it is not therefore an automatic sit but a command or signal sit. You may choose either alternative according to your own thoughts.

If I am walking my dog and stop frequently to look into shop windows, I do not expect my companion to automatically sit when I

might move on just a few seconds later. To me, this is an example of effecting a drill for its own sake. As long as my dog stands still when I come to a halt, this is satisfactory. However, if I want the dog to sit, I will simply give the slightest of

An Australian Shepherd at HEEL. The dog is Blue Lad Michigan Bobby owned by Scott George.

tugs on the lead and it will know I want it to sit. With practice you will find that the dog can all but read your mind and is able to sense the very slightest movement in the way you handle the lead when you come to a halt.

To train your puppy for the heel and sit, it is simply a case of saying sit every time you come to a halt. At the same time, give a slight upward and backward tug on the lead. It should not be a jerk if the puppy already understands the command sit. With a young puppy you may need to adjust the position it takes up because some will otherwise sit in a rather sloppy sideways position. Once the pup gets the general idea, you can actually maneuver it by the using the lead in order to move it forward a little if need be.

If the puppy does not sit, you should hold its collar with your right hand while pressing its rump with your left hand and say sit in a quiet but firm voice. With regular practice you will find that you can drop the verbal command and the pup should take up the sit position each time you stop. I teach my pups to sit on a command, but will practice walking and then stopping without issuing the command. They will often automatically sit at first, but as they grow older they will

This is a magnificent Standard Schnauzer puppy. It is a medium-sized breed and magnificent because it is so well disciplined at this age. Having learned the SIT command so well, this dog can go on to many more disciplines. Owner, Koehl Liwe.

Reward success every time! Whenever your dog executes a command properly, give it appropriate praise. Don't overdo the praise and start a game or else the dog won't differentiate between work time and playtime. The owner of this English Springer Spaniel is Kathy Kirk.

get back to the original position. If the pup attempts to get up and turn around it must be told to sit, then stay in a firmer voice. It can by all means follow your movement with its head as long as it stays in position. This would be a wholly natural thing for it to do because it obviously wants to keep its eyes on you. Next, give the stay command and move forward two paces. You will of course let the lead trail behind you so it is not pulling at the puppy. If it attempts to follow, say stay in a firmer voice. As with the original stay command, when you first taught this to the pup, you should progressively move further away. You will eventually take the lead off so you can walk further away. On the command Rover or come (I prefer to simply call the dog's name), you should tap your left knee so the pup comes and takes up its heel position, either standing, or with an automatic sit, depending on how you have taught the pup to respond to this position. If you wish to use a hand signal for the heel and stay, you should place your hand down in front of the pup's nose, and palm toward this, as you give the stay command. With regular practice the puppy will eventually stay purely on the hand signal.

HEEL FROM RECALL
When you are calling your puppy from the distance stay position, it should come to you on your right-hand side, pass around your back, and take up the heel position to your left. This is smooth and brings the pup into the correct heel position. If this is not done, the pup will maybe return on your

tend to decide for themselves whether they wish to sit or not. I only insist they sit when they are given a lead check or the verbal command.

HEEL AND STAY
There are very few occasions when you would actually wish to use the heel and stay exercise unless in a competitive framework. But it is nonetheless a useful thing for your puppy to understand. It must of course already understand the sit and stay commands.

To teach this command you bring the puppy to the heel and sit position and then say stay. Move to your right and walk around your puppy until you left side and must then be maneuvered into the heel position. This is clumsy. The way to teach the puppy to move behind you when it is approaching you from the front is as follows:

Place the pup in front of you on its lead and in the sit and stay position. Now tell it to heel. As it moves toward you, take your right hand and guide the lead around your back, changing the lead to your left

of you and into position; then praise it.

RECALL, FRONT SIT AND HEEL

A variation on the recall and heel that will be needed in obedience and retriever training, but which is useful even if you are only throwing a stick or a Frisbee™ for your puppy to fetch, is the front sit and heel after a recall. To teach this you can again start with the pup on a lead in the sit

heel. You can in fact have an option of whether the pup is to return to sit in front of you, or to go straight behind you without the front sit. First teach it the front sit then, when you give the heel command, you hold your arm out at a downward angle, with your index finger extended. Make a sweeping arc to your right as you say heel.

With practice you can then send the puppy straight to the heel by using the arm signal as it approaches you. Of course, you still use the voice commandheel. Initially, it may take the pup a while to grasp this, but if you persevere, success will come. You can

COME is the most important command you can teach your dog. If ever walking offlead (or if accidentally off his lead), your dog will respond and possibly keep him from harm (oncoming traffic, bikers, other dogs).

Roz Mooney owns this "beggar"! A well-trained puppy can sit for a long time (a minute or two) in the begging pose. Because they are usually rewarded when holding this pose, most puppies learn to beg easily.

hand as it passes behind you and into the heel. If it tries to go to your left you must pull it around to your right. Practice this a number of times and the required action will be effected. When this has been done satisfactorily a number of times, try it with the puppy further away and offlead.

If it moves to your right, simply get hold of its collar and pull the pup around the back

position some feet in front of you. Call the pup and as it reaches you, tell it to sit. Hold this position for a few seconds before giving the heel command, using the lead to guide it around the back of you.

If you plan to have your dog return to you in this manner, then you should teach it to come in front of you every time from the outset of recalling to also use a hand signal if you wish to give the pup extra help in deciding which way to return to you. For the recall and sit, you will hold your right arm down straight in front of you, with the index finger pointing to a spot between your front feet.

Learning these heel-related commands is somewhat more

is seen in working, field, obedience or agility competitions around the country.

In teaching your dog basic obedience, do not assume that once taught the dog will never again need to practice. Naturally, you will use a number of the commands during day-to-day exercising

standard, there will be a tendency for these to regress, just as any athlete will not maintain peak performance unless he or she practices on a regular schedule.

The practice need only take a few minutes and you can even make a game of it. What I will do when taking any of my dogs for a run in a park or in the country is so quick and simple that they are not even aware they are reviewing their formal training. When I get to the park, I will find a quiet spot and then take them offlead. I do not issue one single voice command but run through all their basic obedience rapidly by using hand signals.

I start by releasing the lead and then using a sweeping arc to bring the dog straight around my back into the heel and sit. Then I point to my toes and the dog will move to the front sit. Next is a quick beg by raising my fingers just above the dog's head. From here it is a hand arc back around me to the heel and stay position. Now I walk about 20 paces forward and without turning my head I will pat my left knee, which brings the dog into the heel. Next we will do a forward walk with a right turn, then a left, and then an about-turn. Next there is the hand signal to heel and stay as I walk away a few paces before turning to the dog.

Now I give the down hand signal, then the up to the sit (which is simply raising the hand from low to high—the reverse of the down). Now another recall to the front sit and we end by the dog rolling over by my using my finger to quickly draw a circle in the air

A lovely Dalmatian demonstrates GIVE ME YOUR PAW. Every dog must be reminded of its training by repetition. Repetition is the mother of all training.

advanced than the average pet puppy is taught. But they are still relatively simple commands when compared to what a dog can learn if it is trained to do the sort of advanced obedience work that

of the dog, but you should make a point of periodically testing your dog on all commands so they do not become rusty. Without continually monitoring that your pet is retaining a given

Using a safe Gumabone® dental device (chew toy), this smart German Shepherd won't move unless her mistress calls or signals. Nobody else, regardless of their call or signal, can get this well-trained dog to budge.

Above: Magnificent mother and daughter Belgian Sheepdogs, well trained to sit and stay, take a moment to say "Hi!"

Left: Golden Retriever puppies almost ready to start training. Before ever scolding a puppy, be sure you have established a strong, loving bond of trust and respect.

in front of the dog. Finally comes the first use of the voice with "there's a good boy" and lots of fuss. The dog will jump up and down in an excited manner and I will then say "go on then," and it is away in a big sweeping fun run. The exercises have become a game to the dog and really are completed at high speed and in great spirits. There is no need for commands to become mundane and boring rituals unless you make them become this. In teaching your puppy to understand basic commands, you will find that you too will be the better for this. You will be more aware of the importance of controlling your puppy, and this will rub off in the way you go about teaching it to be good around the home. You will not only set standards for the pup but you will be setting standards for yourself. The result will be a much happier bonding with your dog and a pet that matures without any psychological problems or hangups.

Your puppy, regardless of his pedigree or breed, is still a very intelligent animal. The most obedient and clever dog I ever owned was not a German Shepherd nor a Rottweiler but a little crossbred terrier that had an incredible ability to learn tricks and retain commands and signals. Your pup's powers of learning are far greater than most other pets. This means it needs to learn things to keep its mind healthy and active. A bored mind can only result in mischief in one form or another, because the dog's brain must have some outlet for its capacity. In this sense it is comparable to the human child. If a child is not taught the difference between right and wrong, it is more likely to become delinquent.

Never use hard discipline when teaching your puppy basic commands because it can learn with minimal corrections. The word no should not be needed in this area of training. Use that for teaching it what it must not do around the home. For basic commands to be learned well, you should always strive to keep things as simple as possible. I would also recommend you to use hand signals because once taught to your puppy they do save needless shouting and wasted conversation that is all too common with many people who get too wrapped up in voice commands. Your puppy is extremely observant. When in the wild, pups will learn far more from observing facial and body movements in other animals, and their own kind, than by actual vocal sounds. Your pup learns much from body language—always use your arms and hands to their natural advantages. With patience and understanding, you will soon have an admirable and obedient dog with whom you share a very special bond.

This Golden Retriever, whose name is Sharlow's Irish Sundancer and who is owned by Dan and Neva Sharlow, is trained to retrieve from the water.

INDEX

SUGGESTED READING

THE BOOKS LISTED BELOW ARE INVALUABLE FOR ASSISTANCE IN TRAINING YOUR DOG. THESE BOOKS ARE AVAILABLE AT MOST PET SHOPS. OBVIOUSLY YOU SHOULD HAVE A BOOK ON YOUR BREED AS EACH BREED OF DOG HAS ITS OWN INDIVIDUALITIES.

TRAINING BOOKS FROM T.F.H. PUBLICATIONS, INC.

EVERYBODY CAN TRAIN THEIR OWN DOG
By Angela White
TW-113
Hardcovered, 5 x 7, 256 pages, 200 color photos.

SUCCESSFUL DOG TRAINING
By Michael Kramer, OSB
TS-205
Hardcovered, 7 x 12, 160 pages, over 150 color photographs.

JUST SAY "GOOD DOG"
By Linda Goodman and Marlene Trunnell
TS-204
Softcover, 5 1/2 x 8 1/2, 192 pages, original cartoons.

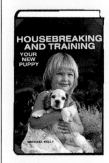

HOUSE-BREAKING YOUR NEW PUPPY
By Michael Kelly
TU-011
Softcovered, 7 x 8 1/2, 64 pages, full color photographs.

HOUSE-BREAKING YOUR PUPPY, STEP BY STEP
By Jack C. Harris
SK-025
Softcovered, 5 1/2 x 8 1/2, 64 pages, over 50 color photos.

CHILDREN'S GUIDE TO DOG TRAINING
By Denise P. Cherry
SK-044
Softcovered, 5 1/2 x 8 1/2, 64 pages, 60 color photographs.

BASIC DOG TRAINING
By Miller Watson
KW-022
Hardcovered, 5 x 8 1/2, 96 pages, over 100 color photographs.

DOG TRAINING BY LEW BURKE
By Lew Burke
Hardcovered, 5 1/2 x 8 1/2, 255 pages, over 60 color photographs.

Acknowledgment

This volume in the *Basic Domestic Pet Library* series was researched in part at the Ontario Veterinary college at the University of Guelph in Guelph, Ontario, and was published under the auspice of Dr. Herbert R. Axelrod.

A world-renown scientist, explorer, author, university professor, lecturer, and publisher, Dr. Axelrod is the best-known tropical fish expert in the world and the founder and chairman of T.F.H. Publications, Inc., the largest and most respected publisher of pet literature in the world. He has written 16 definitive texts on Ichthyology (including the bestselling *Handbook of Tropical Aquarium Fishes*), published more than 30 books on individual species of fish for the hobbyist, written hundreds of articles, and discovered hundreds of previously unknown species, six of which have been named after him.

Dr. Axelrod holds a Ph.D and was awarded an Honorary Doctor of Science degree by the University of Guelph, where he is now an adjunct professor in the Department of Zoology. He has served on the American Pet Products Manufacturers Association Board of Governors and is a member of the American Society of Herpetologists and Ichthyologists, the Biometric Society, the New York Zoological Society, the New York Academy of Sciences, the American Fisheries Society, the National Research Council, the National Academy of Sciences, and numerous aquarium societies around the world.

In 1977, Dr. Axelrod was awarded the Smithson Silver Medal for his ichthyological and charitable endeavors by the Smithsonian Institution. A decade later, he was elected an endowment member of the American Museum of Natural History and was named a life member of the James Smithson Society by the Smithsonian Associates' national board. He has donated in excess of $50 million in recent years to the American Museum of National History, the University of Guelph, and other institutions.